Social Knowledge:
Organizational Currencies in the New Knowledge Economy

The Definitive Guide to Social Knowledge Management

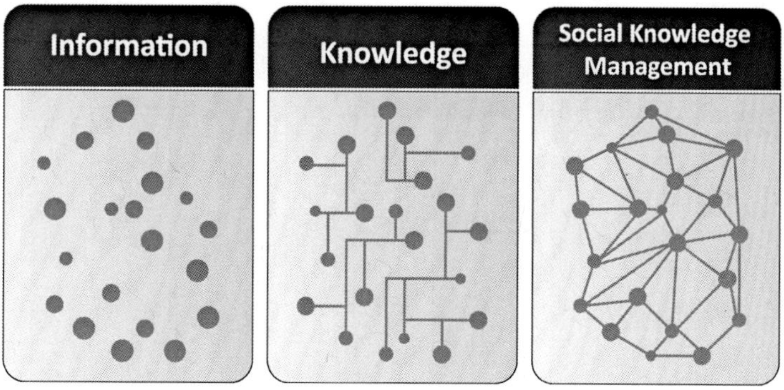

Kenneth E Russell, PhD

Renée La Londe

Fred Walters

Spencer House Publishing

September 2014

ISBN: Hardback 978-0-692-28477-3

Paperback 978-0-692-28478-0

Contents

Dedications

Ken Russell:

I'd like to thank my family (particularly my wife Ann, and our children: Christian and Alison) for allowing me to continue the journey I started so long ago. Without their support, and the support of my co-authors, colleagues and friends, I wouldn't be able to do what I do.

legatum ex nihilo

Renée La Londe:

To the amazing guys that bring so much love to my life:
Doug and Toot (Reedin).

Fred Walters:

To the girls that bring joy to my life: Lori and Charli.

From us all:

To all the folks at iTalent and
the Intellectual Capital Transformation Team at Cisco:
il miglior fabbro!

Foreword

A few years back we were facing what most would consider a "Knowledge Management" problem: how to accelerate the knowledge and expertise of over 3,500 technical support engineers. These individuals were located throughout the world - in 17 countries, using about 25 different approaches with different case management systems. Why was that a problem? The industry average to create such an expert engineer is over five years. Our challenge was to find a way to accelerate the development curve so we could "reduce the time to expert" and get qualified and experienced talent in front of our customers. . . and each other . . . quickly. We could not rely on the "old fashioned" methods, including sitting a new engineer next to a seasoned pro and just waiting for the experiences to transfer by osmosis.

We had to think differently – smarter, quicker and value driven. We had to think Social.

We started first with the idea of Intelligent Matching, what many call "precision routing" in the technical support world. Essentially, we wanted to make sure our experts were more readily reachable. Think about any time you call in for support and are redirected (or "escalated") to another resource. We did not want that to be standard practice for our customers.

While we were at it, we discovered we could be much more collaborative and bi-directional with our approach to connecting our experts with each other. Who better to work with and determine any knowledge gaps in a technical support engineer than with another engineer? Instead of merely routing to an expert, we added a "click to collaborate" option that enabled learning opportunities for both our customers and our technical support engineers.

Collaboration is driving a consumption-based knowledge economics engine in our company. As a knowledge asset is consumed, the reputation of that piece of knowledge grows. Based on this consumption model, we know two things: First, we are stamping a reputation on the asset so it becomes very clear whether it can be valued or not. Second, the reputation drives our engineer "leader board"; good stuff rises and the not-so good falls off.

In the end, we implemented an award-winning, global, borderless technical support organization where skills-based inventory, skills-based routing, a reputation engine, and interactive collaboration through gamification became embedded into our normal, everyday workflow. Our approach leveraged the Social Knowledge of our technical support organization in ways that not only changed how we created knowledge… . . . but how we consumed it as well.

I welcome you to take the time to read this book, consider the possibilities, and know that Social Knowledge can be a powerful asset for your company. Not only do we now know how quickly our engineers can become experts, we know what they know, how much they know, when they learned it, and (more importantly) what our other experts think of them . . . all in real time!

Sincerely,

Vijay Bollapragada
Senior Director
Cisco, Inc.

Foreword

A true story of social knowledge shows why it matters: A large firm branched into biofuels processing in Argentina[1]. Unfortunately, its processes also produced combustible dust as a byproduct, not something you want around fuel. Local engineers could not solve the problem; neither could the lead engineers based in London. A social process identified an engineer in Australia who knew the answer, saving the firm not only millions of dollars but also reducing its risk and potentially saving lives.

Social knowledge will give you two kinds of insights: knowledge of your community and knowledge about your community. The first is important because it will help you find and develop expertise. The second is important because it will help you wield influence. Effective executives need both and this book tells you how.

Written by experts with decades of experience, this book provides the insights to bring social knowledge to your firm. The authors identify five types of organizational currency, which provide key performance indicators (KPIs) to help you measure and track progress. Using the metaphor of a journey, they provide a roadmap to avoid the potholes and reach the pinnacles of successful knowledge management. Topics include mobile collaboration, wikis and blogs, enterprise software, and dynamic communities that retain and reuse information. Social Knowledge covers not just processes and technology but also people. Many organizations focus

1 Benbya, H. and Van Alstyne, M. How to Find Answers Within Your Company, MIT Sloan Management Review Vol. 52 #2, Cambridge, MA.

on process and more organizations focus on technology but only the great ones also develop their people.

Given such lofty goals, the question always arises as to whether such techniques work. An MIT study at the Center for Digital Business[2] examined the information sharing practices of a Japanese bank and found that social practices such as those articulated here increased productivity as much as 10 percent. What would you do with an extra 25 days of output each year?

Read this book to give yourself that option.

Sincerely,

Marshall Van Alstyne, PhD
Associate Professor Boston University
Research Scientist, MIT Center for Digital Business

---

2 Di Maggio, M. and Van Alstyne, M. Information Sharing, Social Norms and Performance, MIT Center for Digital Business, Cambridge, MA.

Chapter 1 – The Odometer Reading: Evolution of Social Knowledge Management

Social Knowledge simply stated is the information created through interaction. When people communicate to formulate ideas or solve problems, valuable knowledge is generated. This is not new; it has been around forever. However, with the emergence of social networking there is a new convergence of technologies, capabilities, human behaviors, and expectations that are changing the landscape and how we interact with each other, our customers, our partners, and especially our business colleagues and peers. **Social Knowledge Management™ (SKM)** as a practice works to facilitate and demonstrate how knowledge assets can be (re) used effectively and contributes to the success of communicating within connected organizations. It has and will continue to reshape how we live, work, and play. Our social knowledge, then, is a key factor in a larger *Social Knowledge Economy* that governs our approach to working together, how we go to market, and how we exist in a collaborative society powered by interactive technologies - making social knowledge critical in the vocabulary of today's thought leaders. But why is social knowledge so valuable and so different from established knowledge management practices? A brief evolutionary history will provide the backdrop for why social knowledge is so important and relevant in today's fast-paced enterprise.

Conversations Build Communities

Social Knowledge emerges out of both formal (company meetings, portals, and email), as well as informal (office communications and reliance on chance encounters) conversations and the incidental sharing of information commonly known as *tribal knowledge.* Whether formal or informal, Social Knowledge has, at its core, the very basic elements of human interaction: the conversation. Think about what a conversation is: it is *bidirectional,* it is *participatory,* and it is *informational.* Social Knowledge is all of these things plus a bit of technology that enables conversations to take place between different individuals, whether they are across the building or across the world. There is a synergy that occurs through the *culmination of these ideas* that work together to create and build communities.

Isn't social knowledge the same as everyday conversation? Isn't participating and sharing information just *what we do*?

Think about your everyday life.

Most conversations occur in our lives without specific thought or consideration regarding the essential elements of Social Knowledge Management: Sharing, Tracking, Crediting, and Retaining. These elements hint at an *organizational currency* (currencies, actually), and each contributes to making Social Knowledge a relevant, influential, and valuable asset within an organization. Below are short definitions of each of the five organizational currencies that we will learn more about in Chapter 4. These are the key elements that represent organizational value in today's *Social Knowledge Economy*:

- **Content (Knowledge Assets):** Provides a way for teams to capture knowledge naturally, thereby creating a *Content* creation cycle where content is created, evolved, and shared globally.
- **Contribution (Credit Tracing):** Provides a way for organizations to track *Contributions* back to the origin of a knowledge asset.
- **Enhanced Human Experience:** Provides a solution that inspires people to participate, create, and socialize.
- **Collaboration (Engagement/Sharing):** Provides opportunities for teams to connect, capture conversations, and *Collaborate* to solve business challenges together.
- **Competence Acceleration (Expert):** Provides for the ability to accelerate *Competence* in the organization by fast-tracking the learning process and helping teams expand the number of subject matter experts quickly.

More Than an Idea, It's a Practice

Social knowledge is challenging boundaries as organizations are being pushed to be more creative and innovative. The resulting activities can lead to ambiguity and chaos as social knowledge capabilities begin to emerge organically across the enterprise. The path to the destination of a thriving SKM practice is transformational; however, it can be treacherous, bumpy, and crowded! Organizations that can harness the practice of Social

Knowledge Management effectively will drive exponential value back into the business.

SKM delivers a distinct practice that provides the framework and method to capture, create, iterate, and share social knowledge assets across organizations. It is the demand to unlock the value that Social Knowledge provides that propels an SKM practice. SKM is the vehicle, Social Knowledge is the engine, and people are the fuel.

An Evolutionary Road

Social Knowledge Management has evolved as part of the advances we have experienced since the proliferation of the World Wide Web (WWW) in the early 1990s. The journey, however, to connect the knowledge workforce has been dramatic.

Consider the last 20 years:

- Web, Intranet, Extranet, and Portals: These platforms focused on Community but did not promote the use of knowledge and had minimal collaboration.
- Knowledge Bases (KBs): These platforms focused on content but did not focus on user-driven communities, limiting collaboration.
- Early On-Demand Customer Relationship Management (OD CRM): Captured problems and tracked issues but lacked robust reuse opportunities.
- Email: Fostered collaboration and *individual* knowledge bases, but remained locked up in email folders with limited external access.

- Early Instant Messaging (IM/Web Support Chat): These have collaboration, but limited retained knowledge.
- Blogs: A step forward in online collaboration but with limited creativity or retention of structured knowledge assets.
- Social Network (Enterprise and Mobile Collaboration): Real-time, anywhere, dynamic collaboration with limited ability to retain and reuse. Enabled creation of robust communities but limited ability to evolve the valuable interactions into knowledge assets.
- Social Knowledge Management: (SKM): This practice converges collaboration, communities, content management, and traditional knowledge management enabling the capture, publication, and reuse of the organization's Intellectual Capital/Property.

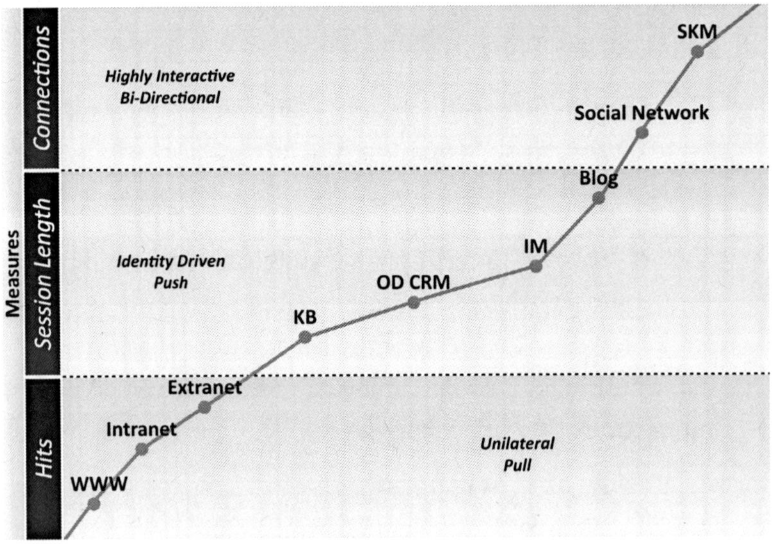

Managing Social Knowledge: People, Process, Technology, and the Human Experience

For business solutions, we historically focus on *people, process*, and *technology*. Many organizations spend a great deal of time on *process* and even more on the *technology*, but very little time on the most important component, the *people*. The *human experience* within an organization is significant, and when enabled by technology, it is a leading factor in the success or failure of any effort or project. An underpinning of the *human experience* is the *organization architecture*, and contributes to the way in which resources are organized to optimize an SKM practice.

Influence of Social Knowledge Management

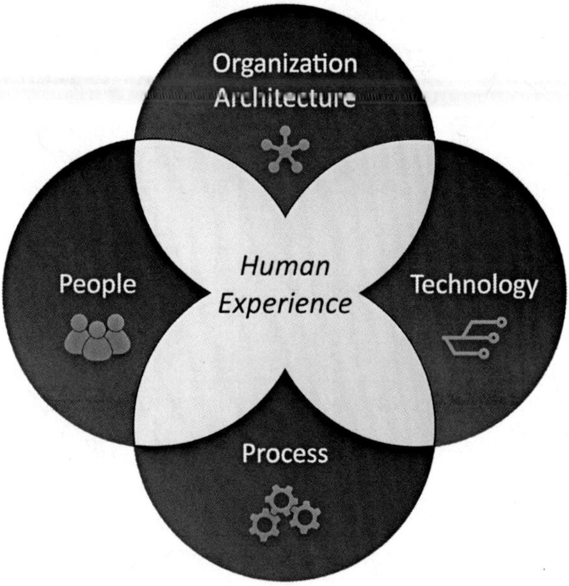

Without the *people* component, *processes* are not pursued and *technology* is not used, and most importantly, knowledge is not created.

Showing Value with SKM (Putting Miles on the Odometer)

Social Knowledge Management (SKM) contributes to the organization in a number of ways. These contributions have measurable value (currency) and can be used as guideposts that help mark progress and maximize the access and benefits of shared knowledge. These include:

- **Meaningful Content:** Creation and capture of valuable collaborative knowledge.
- **Refine and Reuse:** Dynamic interactions to capture, (re) use, iterate, evolve and share knowledge.
- **Expert Acceleration:** Faster development of expert knowledge workers.
- **Acknowledgement:** Enabling the ability to track, recognize, and give accolades.
- **Adoption:** Increasing usage resulting in a more productive, effective and satisfying environment.

Organizations have never been better equipped to maximize the value of knowledge. SKM provides a method, a technique, and an approach to working with human capital in new and more meaningful ways . . . all while turning *normal* collaboration into knowledge that can be captured, shared, and reused. The practice of SKM enables an organization to harness of the value of knowledge from what was once ambiguous and chaotic by leveraging new and emerging technologies, expanded capabilities, and a better understanding and application of the human experience.

Quick List: Are you prepared for the SKM journey?

You will know you are ready for SKM when:

- You can't remember why a particular solution was implemented.
- Your organization solves the same problem, over and over again.
- Your inability to develop experts quickly inhibits the scalability of your organization.
- What knowledge you do have seems to age quickly and is highly perishable.
- You finally realize there needs to be a destination to your journey (not just a constant road trip).
- You leave meetings with lots of notes, but no knowledge.
- You spend a lot of time on process improvement but realize it wasn't the process (or the technology) after all . . . it is the people.

Step by Step: Want to try something today?

Follow these steps to kick off the SKM process:

1. Make a list of all of the *notes* outside your knowledge management system you have to remind you of processes and tasks (check around you as well to see what others are doing).
2. Make sure all processes have a *human element.* Many people tend to skip the need for human participation in a value chain. This is a key element of SKM.

3. Make sure you are on at least two different social media platforms and understand how to use them.

Chapter 2 - Potholes and Detours: Patching, Designing Work-Arounds, or Creating Something New

In the last chapter, you learned the origins of SKM, but whenever a new process is introduced into a new organization, there can be challenges. Before we discuss the actual process, we wanted to address these challenges. When you know what is on the road ahead, you can make proactive decisions rather than reactive ones.

All organizations have processes, systems, relationships, and initiatives that just don't seem to work as planned, or over time they can become misaligned, fractured, or damaged in some way. We call these *potholes* and they present a challenge since a dynamic and growing organization must decide whether to simply *patch* a pothole or avoid the pothole by developing a *work-around.* A work-around can work in the short term, but it rarely solves the underlying problem and usually becomes even more complex than the pothole it was intended to avoid. Ultimately, an organization must take the time to consider the value of a quick patch, a work-around, or simply taking a step back to evaluate the organization's strategy and develop a completely new direction . . . a *NEW road altogether*.

Common Potholes

Organizations maneuver around potholes and various bumps in their evolution or journey every day. Below is a list of the obstacles that are common or are particularly troublesome and warrant consideration as you prepare to leverage social knowledge.

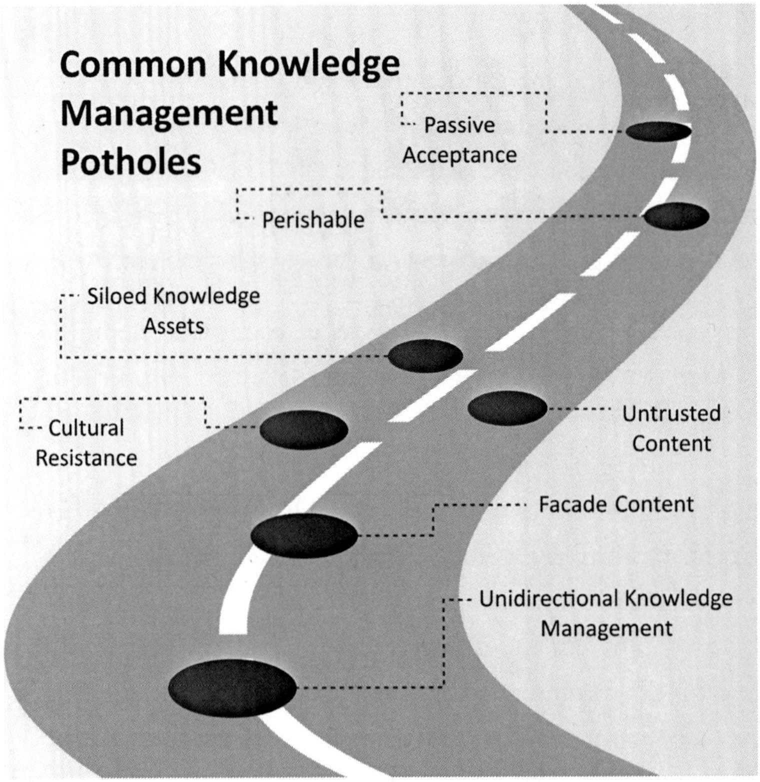

- **Unidirectional Knowledge Management:** Unidirectional knowledge management only works if you have dedicated resources with dedicated time, shared traceability, rewards, and proper management. These same resources must be able to iterate dynamically and improve the knowledge asset within the operational workflow.

- **Facade Content:** Content is assumed valuable but in reality offers little value or is not applicable for the situation or to the knowledge worker.
- **Cultural Resistance or Disenchantment:** An organization's business culture does not support the open sharing of knowledge assets or there have been repeated attempts to implement similar shared knowledge strategies unsuccessfully and teams are (understandably) skeptical of the possibility of success.
- **Untrusted Content:** The knowledge captured is either aged, incomplete, inaccurate, does not address real-world needs, or otherwise suspect. Content (and maybe even the process used to capture and iterate knowledge) is in question and not generally considered dependable.
- **Siloed Knowledge Assets:** Different and disparate solutions to solve local knowledge sharing requirements without a globally integrated strategy or approach.
- **Perishable:** The lifespan of knowledge assets in today's fast-paced environment is limited and can age quickly if not effectively managed. Value begins to decline at the point of creation if the asset is not maintained and updated appropriately.

- **Passive Acceptance:** Key activities to support the Social Knowledge Management Environment (SKME) and the adoption process have limited success due to tacit agreement without fully understanding the scope of knowledge management efforts. Assets become orphaned, misaligned, or contextually obsolete as they are not effectively managed on an ongoing basis.

Why the Potholes Often Don't Get Patched

Gaps and potholes can be obvious or hidden. The challenge is in being prepared for them and, more importantly, understanding why they don't get fixed. Patching the pothole or narrowing a gap can seem like a basic task but other activities may impact the ability to isolate and address the potholes. As you prepare for an SKM journey, be aware it is not just about the road or the supplies needed for the trip, *consider all the detours and potholes* you'll encounter along the way. Some common rationalizations as to why potholes are not patched:

- **Lack of Management Support**: Without the adoption of a corporate-wide collaboration and knowledge strategy by upper management, filling the gaps in knowledge use and retention is destined for failure. *Buy-in* from all levels of management is critical. Lack of buy-in can occur when a decision-maker fails to see particular benefit from social knowledge efforts, or worse, becomes convinced it is a fad. There has to be agreement and support from the top down; moreover, having an executive champion will provide a channel to effectively represent the benefits and investments required to continue the SKM journey.

- **Questionable Value:** There must be positive value for the organization's strategies, goals, and vision. Alignment to specific key performance indicators (KPIs) or other measurements must be identified and tracked. Value can become questionable if strategies are either prematurely conveyed or if they lack proper alignment with results. This can result in misaligned expectations and outcomes.

- **Limited Participation:** Respected resources are not engaged *early and often* in the Social Knowledge process; most importantly ownership (or perceived ownership) does not occur. Lacking the influence of senior stakeholders prevents the optimal dialogue necessary for successful implementations.

- **Knowledge Guarding:** Conflict between the *old school* knowledge gatekeeper fraternity and the newer knowledge workers creates an uncomfortable sharing environment, which inhibits *knowledge through collaboration*. This is very much a cultural shift and should be considered as part of your change management efforts.

- **Behavioral Change**: Tangible knowledge assets don't usually emerge out of traditional collaboration. Demonstrating the benefit of sharing, capturing, retaining, and publishing knowledge and how it makes everyone's work better can be difficult and time consuming.

- **Noise:** Trying to capture too much content can drown out and dilute valuable contributions. Focusing too much on interactions associated with initiatives rather than the knowledge assets can result in an environment where it's difficult to discern value.

The Fallacy of the Work-Around

The trouble with potholes is they create a call to action within organizations to *just fix* them. Unfortunately, fixing a pothole without fully understanding the underlying issues that caused the damage in the first place can be a futile effort. We have a good understanding of what causes potholes, as well as why they don't get fixed; now it is time to turn our attention to the work-around.

One of the tenets of human behavior is that people tend to gravitate to what they know. As an example, we are more likely to continue using the same worn-out, pothole-filled, roadway even though there may be a new damage-free expressway one block over. Why? We are indeed creatures of habit. In social knowledge terms, we follow patterns. We'd much rather use the same wobbly keyboard, or the cracked coffee mug, or use the *more comfortable* instant messaging software. Think of the uproar when your favorite social media software or service announces a new update.

Work-Arounds Can Obscure the Big Picture

Work-arounds start out simply enough. They are intended to avoid, get past, circumnavigate, or just avoid a pothole. Sometimes work-arounds happen without much thought, such as just stepping over or around the damage. This would be like having to deal with a few extra mouse clicks to get access to the free Wi-Fi at the airport, or using your keyboard shortcut because you forgot your mouse. But work-arounds can be very complex, too. Consider the *Unidirectional Knowledge Management* pothole mentioned earlier:

> A good example of how a work-around can become complex is when multiple business locations develop their own solutions instead of working together on a common approach. Although perhaps inefficient, everyone is happy, until something breaks the process. In the chaos that ensues after a process is broken (a pothole), the natural human behavior proclivity is just to get past it and move on. In our example, each location creates new policies and processes to get around the damage (knowledge is created but not shared or iterated). Without a cohesive strategy to bring the disparate sites together several unique work-arounds are created when *one could have done the trick.*

Let's consider the same example, this time influenced by a Social Knowledge Management Strategy/Environment. Using an SKM strategy, work-arounds would not have been created in silos. Instead, an analysis of what happened, and why it happened would be shared and a robust remediation plan would be developed and leveraged for the entire organization:

> Multiple business locations, leveraging a Social Knowledge Management Environment (SKME) to communicate, collaborate, and share knowledge become aware of a broken process and immediately communicate the information. The resulting knowledge asset is recognized (thumbs up, like, or kudo) and team members begin discussing the best course

of action to address the damaged process. Good ideas rise up in the rankings in the discussion while less popular postings fall to the bottom. A collaborative solution is determined, a record of the activities is documented, and business continues with barely a bump.

As mentioned earlier, being prepared for your SKM journey is critical. It's not just the damaged road to consider but the *human behaviors* that influence what happens after a pothole (or a work-around) emerges.

Take a Moment to Consider the NEW Road

What about the new expressway that just opened up? As mentioned earlier, we tend to gravitate to what is *known* or *comfortable*. Even when a new path is available (or a new system, or process, or social knowledge environment) we tend to prefer the *tried and true*, the *standard*, or *what everyone else is doing*. It's important to take a moment, lift your head above the fray of everyday life, and take time to consider new possibilities.

Imagine what we would have missed if we:

- Kept using *dial up,*
- Didn't have the ability to *move between multiple windows* on our computer, or
- Avoided Facebook, LinkedIn, or Twitter because they *impact your privacy.*

The point is that new roads are meant for driving! When considering your Social Knowledge Management journey, remember the most important thing is to *begin!*

Quick List: When is it time for a new path?

You are ready for SKM when:

- You can't tell the difference between a patch and a work-around.
- A work-around has a work-around.
- You have to stop and evaluate how much time is being spent on the work-around as opposed to moving to a new process.
- The upfront time and resource investment for a new path seems like a great idea (Hint: *It was probably a good idea much earlier than you may have observed.*).

Step by Step: Want to try something today?

Follow this process:

1. Make a list of all potholes and work-arounds your company is currently facing relative to your knowledge asset management process.
2. Determine the value (prioritize by process, by use, or anything that shows the value).
3. Determine any overlap.
4. Decide if the pothole or work-around is still needed. Can it all be *paved over*?

Chapter 3 – On the Road: Moving Toward your Own Social Knowledge Management Platform

When an organization evaluates a shift from a current state to a new way of operating, it is typically driven from the top down in order to align to a goal(s) that is key to that organization's overall success. We will consider SKM in light of focus areas including, but not limited to, the following:

- Enhanced Customer Experience
- Enhanced Partner/Channel Experience
- Improved Customer Support
- Improved Sales and Marketing Productivity
- Enhanced Cross-Functional Collaboration
- (and of critical importance) Trust in the Knowledge

Most likely, you've already had exposure to a full suite of business applications (including Knowledge Management tools) and you have hit potholes similar to what we reviewed in Chapter 2: Unidirectional Knowledge Management, "Facade" Content, Siloed Knowledge Assets, Perishable, Passive Acceptance, and Untrusted Content. Any one of those potholes can slow down a change management effort, so how do you make a shift?

You will know your organization is ready to make the adjustments required to pave a new road when your organization has:

- Recognized the value of collaborative knowledge lost
- Grown tired of dealing with the frustration of myriad lost opportunities to impact client satisfaction
- Gained management alignment and support
- Garnered active participation by internal influential subject matter experts
- Reached clarity of purpose, including understanding the impact of SKM capabilities
- Defined measureable value around SKM

In this chapter, we will review the powerful role Social Knowledge Management plays within organizations and the breakthroughs teams experience when Social Knowledge Management Environments are implemented.

Before we begin, let's quickly review how SKM is different from other Knowledge Management efforts. One well-known example is Knowledge-Center Support (KCS). At first glance SKM and KCS may seem similar (especially from the perspective of a technical support scenario). While the goals and objectives may be similar, the process and methodology (the journey) is different. SKM is the convergence of Enterprise Interactions (Collaboration), Knowledge Management, and Content Management. Social Knowledge, as the name suggests, starts with the social interactions and evolves them to knowledge assets. KCS begins a bit differently, with traditional knowledge and incident management processes and methodologies. These are not mutually exclusive activities; in fact, the initiatives should be aligned and integrated (converged).

A comprehensive social strategy, both internally and externally, is critically important as a majority of knowledge originates with social interaction. Social Knowledge Management provides an end-to-end view of knowledge within an enterprise. The risk of considering only Knowledge and Incident Management without considering Social can lead to a potential loss of knowledge assets. Such assets would be more readily apparent in an SKM environment; whereas, the same assets would be more difficult to identify or discover in a traditional knowledge management environment. KCS users typically have a single destination environment available for updating content and just adding a social component, such as chat, is not enough. It must be a collaborative environment, with multiple access and iteration points. If your organization has a KCS methodology in place, it is important to consider SKM as a catalyst to incorporating social elements as a practice to capture and help iterate potentially critical, valuable knowledge.

Information is power. It's a popular message but *it's no longer what your organization knows that brings value to your company. It is your organization's ability to share what you know* with others that truly makes it a powerful force in the work place. Taking the step to unleash the benefits of a social knowledge organizational currencies (Content, Collaboration, Contribution, Competence and Enhance Human Experience) contained within your team, department, or organization are the foundational elements of

SKM. Today's organization is measured based on the value of the content it produces, the information it shares, the impact it has, the expertise it provides, and the overall ease in which it delivers value to respective clients.

Guiding the Way

As your organization evaluates opportunities for adopting Social Knowledge Management, consider the following four key business drivers:

- **Solving Problems:** What problem are you solving?

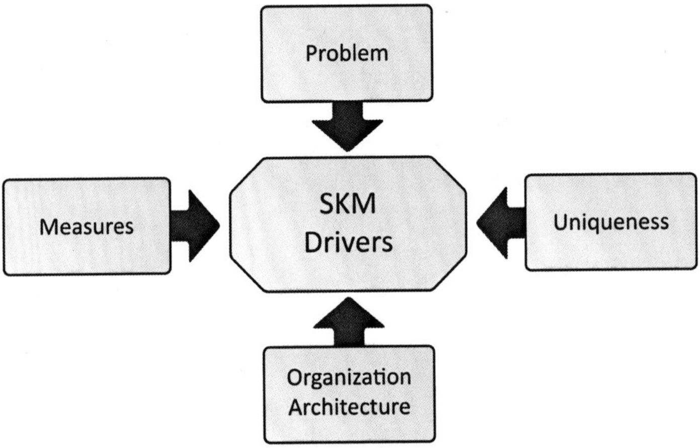

How does the challenge you are trying to solve align to corporate goals? Do you have management alignment and support? Are you replacing or extending an existing capability?

- **Return On Investment (ROI)/Tracking/Metrics:** As your primary activity, evaluate how SKM will bring tangible and intangible benefits (organizational currencies). Consider the impact of factors such as cost savings, increasing sales, and customer satisfaction on the success of the organization. It is important not only to consider *activity* success metrics, but also the *business* success metrics related to financial, satisfaction, and productivity metrics.

- **Organization Architecture:** Do you have the organization architecture in place to support the effort? Is there a sincere understanding of the organization's history, culture, and tolerance for change? What is the high-level change magnitude/impact?

- **Company Uniqueness:** What is it about your organization's characteristics that make it special? Is the uniqueness of your organization (and associated distinct opportunities) reflected in your SKM strategy?

The assessment of these business drivers will help determine the scope, areas of investment, and focus of your SKM strategy. It is important to understand the organizational readiness required to adopt the necessary changes, and identify where there are gaps and how to fill them.

Just as we looked at *what* SKM is earlier, it's time to consider *where* SKM environments can make a difference within your organization, department or team.

Social Knowledge Management Environments (SKMEs) enable users to have real-time conversations that lead to the creation of knowledge assets. These assets are captured within the environment, developed over time through collaboration, and most importantly, are shared and reused by teams across the organization.

This process contributes to the development of a robust social *knowledge economy*—–-an economy where businesses capture the output of human capital and maximize the value of this content into measureable intellectual property and corporate knowledge, enabling a rapid transformation to products and services for customers and partners.

Let's also review *how* SKM can solve complex business problems where disparate traditional knowledge management tools such as KM Applications, Customer Relationship Management (CRM), Email, and Collaboration tools can fall short.

Capabilities and Currencies

Social Knowledge Management has emerged as a result of the dynamic nature of evolving capabilities within enterprise business systems. As depicted in the graphic below and explained in more detail in the following section, Knowledge Management, Enterprise Interactions/Collaboration, and Content Management have converged (inward arrows) as key elements of SKM.

SKM Capabilities and Currencies

As a new practice in the enterprise, Social Knowledge Management creates tangible benefits/currencies (outward facing arrows) that contribute to the overall value of the organization. These include Content/Knowledge Asset, Contribution/Credit Tracing, Enhanced Human Experience, Collaboration/Sharing Knowledge, and Competence/Expert Acceleration.

Both the converging capabilities and benefits/currencies will be explained in more detail in the following sections.

Converging Capabilities

A successful SKM practice requires an understanding of three traditional, yet converging capabilities that are the catalysts that enable an organization to realize and leverage the benefits of new organizational currencies.

- **Knowledge Management:** The *process* of capturing, developing, distributing, and effectively using organizational knowledge.
- **Enterprise Interaction:** The act of working with another person or group in order to *achieve a shared organizational goal.* This can be done through any number of interactive mechanisms (i.e. Instant Messaging, Email, hallway discussions, and discussion boards).
- **Content Management:** The set of processes and technologies that *support* the collection, managing, and publishing of information in any form or medium.

Social Knowledge is about *the creation, retention, iteration, and sharing of knowledge across the enterprise.* You are not able to do this with any one of these capabilities; it is only through the convergence of these capabilities that this is possible.

SKM Capabilities

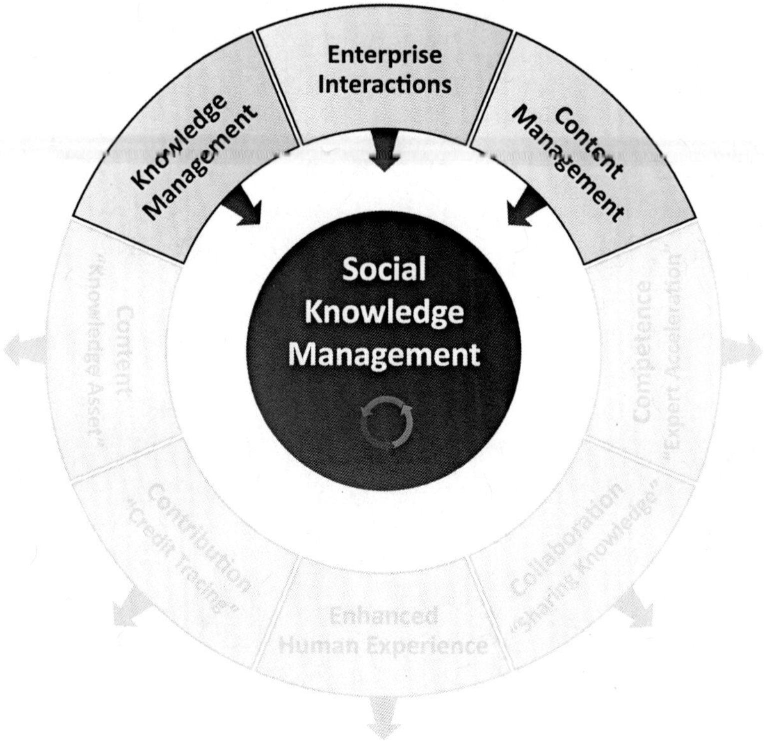

Each of these capabilities influences Social Knowledge Management in very different, but complementary ways. Each is critical for an effective and scalable SKM practice. Moreover, through this convergence the enterprise is able to reap the rewards of new organizational currencies. First, let's understand how each of these disciplines contributes to the capabilities of a Social Knowledge Management Environment (SKME).

- **Knowledge Management:** Although KM has evolved from a more static and less dynamic practice, it is still considered a destination capability in which interacting requires accessing a system (or system of records), rather than leveraging a deep integration with interactive, dynamic, or social capabilities. As noted earlier, Knowledge-Centered Support is a good example of a complementary process that has a robust KM process and methodology, making it a great candidate to integrate with the social mechanisms of SKM.
- **Enterprise Interaction** enables individuals and teams within organizations to connect in order to share thoughts and ideas. However, conversations and interactions alone do not provide an effective method to retain these interactions in a way that make them (re) usable.
- **Content Management** is known for its highly-structured content lifecycle process but limited collaborative capabilities. Knowledge assets produced via SKM are very dynamic and consumed internally and externally. It is important that a robust yet agile content management process is integrated to ensure quality output.

Now that we have reviewed and considered the capabilities that create the catalyst for SKM, let us now consider the organizational currencies that become evident via this convergence.

Organizational Currencies

Below are five organizational currencies (Content, Contribution, Enhance Human Experience, Collaboration, and Competence) that outline *how* Social Knowledge Management helps organizations create and maximize value:

Content (Knowledge Assets)

The first currency of SKM provides a way for teams to capture knowledge naturally, thereby creating a *Content* creation cycle where content is created, evolved, and shared globally.

In the world of SKM, content is dynamic, changing as teams identify and address business challenges in the organization. As content is refined, it increases in value and usefulness. Social Knowledge Management uses *the crowd* to identify and address business challenges in the organization rapidly, while continuing to create and iterate knowledge assets.

The process is simple. Conversations between knowledge workers are captured as content in a Social Knowledge Management environment, in the form of discussions and articles. Everyone with access to the environment is empowered to contribute, refine, and enhance the knowledge. As content is captured, other knowledge workers can search, access, and reuse available content to discover solutions to business challenges.

To help identify great content, knowledge workers are encouraged to rate content for its usefulness. This gives encouragement to authors and contributors to continue creating great content and allows others to identify useful content quickly.

In addition, valuable content is easily flagged and triggers the creation of a more formal knowledge asset that can be published internally and externally.

Activity within Social Knowledge Management is captured via relevant measures and accompanying metrics, which help teams surface valuable and timely knowledge. This helps identify areas where content may need to be refined, refocused, or even archived/ scheduled for additional dispensation.

Contribution (Credit Tracing)

The second breakthrough currency provides a way for organizations to track *Contributions* back to the origin of a knowledge asset. This enables the ability to recognize (including thumbs up, like, kudo) the subject matter experts involved in its creation as well as establishes a provenance of an asset: acknowledging and labeling the conditions surrounding the creation of a knowledge asset while providing an end-to-end history as well.

Many teams experience challenges in identifying who created knowledge, where it exists within their organization, and who has contributed to it during its lifecycle.

Knowledge workers who contribute content and receive high ratings from other users in the Social Knowledge Management Environment can be considered subject matter experts. These experts may now be identified and tapped to assist with specific projects and business initiatives based on their contributions. This introduces the topic of *gamification* and its applicability to a successful SKM strategy. This topic is discussed in Chapter 6, but suffice it to say that incorporating rewards (access) and recognition (badging) within your SKME is important to help drive specific behaviors.

This is more than tagging an interaction or asset with a worker's information. It involves context (why, and for whom it was created/contributed), value (reuse, or deemed valuable by other Social Knowledge workers), and viability (proven, credible Social Knowledge asset).

The measures of success for any worker include reputation, credibility, and contributions to the organization. Because of this, being able to track (or trace) the provenance of a collaboration or origin of a knowledge asset is especially valuable when it comes time to recognize a contributor. Whether in the form of salary, a bonus, or just a pat on the back, social knowledge workers are often well paid in the form of improved reputation and organizational recognition.

Enhanced Human Experience

The third currency of Social Knowledge Management (SKM) is an Enhanced Human Experience. If the solution you are envisioning does not inspire people to participate, create, and socialize, it will not be as successful as a solution that does. Simply, we all want to feel that we are a part of something special. When our contributions are recognized, our opportunities to socialize are increased, and our overall experience with a work effort is amplified (as is the case when leveraging a SKME), then our work product benefits. It should be noted that even if there is a negative experience (a bad rating on a knowledge asset, a difficult conversation, a fractured message) the human experience will still be enhanced, particularly due to the multivariate inputs that lead to an increased corporate memory. Good or bad, the currency of enhanced human behavior is valuable in any dynamic organization.

Enhanced Human Experience

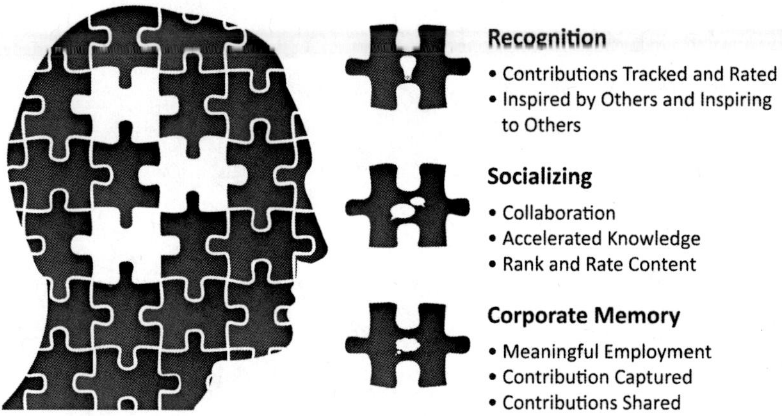

Collaboration (Engagement/Sharing)

The fourth currency of enabling an SKM platform is creating opportunities for teams to *Collaborate* and solve challenges together. Social Knowledge Management connects people and captures their conversations as they collaborate to solve business challenges. It transitions new and experienced knowledge workers from engaging in isolated email or Instant Message conversations to participating in open, collaborative environments where they can capture, create new content, or refine and improve existing content that can be shared with a larger audience. Ideally, this all happens real-time and as a part of the existing workflow. Relevant content is created through collaboration and can be surfaced for reuse when it's needed most.

Competence Acceleration (Expert)

The final currency of SKM is that it accelerates *Competence* in the organization by fast-tracking the learning process and helping teams expand the number of subject matter experts quickly.

Becoming an expert in any field takes time, resources, dedication, and possibly most important - interaction. For Social Knowledge, being able to accelerate an individual's ability to become an expert by increasing the levels of meaningful contextual interactions is crucial.

So how do you quickly ramp up new knowledge workers and turn them into experienced subject matter experts? It's a challenge faced by many organizations. By enabling a Social Knowledge Management Environment (SKME), new knowledge workers have a way to consume, absorb, and contribute to existing knowledge assets created by experts.

If more information is required, new social knowledge workers can simply ask targeted questions to the experts within the SKME. An immediate and active exchange is established between new knowledge workers and more seasoned experts. The SKME creates an opportunity to develop one-to-many or many-to-many (crowd-sourced learning) virtual mentorship relationships in which experts can effectively interact with multiple resources within a particular discipline to maximize learning. The resulting collaboration contributes and iterates existing content and makes it immediately available to everyone in the environment.

Knowledge Workers graduate from being new knowledge workers that consume the knowledge of others, to Social Knowledge Experts who create, contribute, and share knowledge. The *Knowledge Gap* is filled within the SKM environment as knowledge workers are able to easily contribute as well as consume and iterate content.

Now that we have a deeper understanding of the origins and resulting currencies (benefits) of SKM, let's now consider what makes up the SKM platform.

SKM as a Platform

A fully deployed Social Knowledge platform has a broad scope. Below is a view of the business capabilities that can be enabled by deploying a robust but flexible SKM platform. Each of these areas has a critical role in an organization's efforts to source, retain, iterate, or share knowledge. The *challenge* is the work necessary to integrate these capabilities into a seamless and natural workflow process within the enterprise. Expecting a typical knowledge worker to be able to do a wholesale change in the way their job is performed just because you introduce new concepts and possibilities is unrealistic and could be a recipe for failure. *Change* takes time and dedication to new processes. *Transformation* takes that and much more.

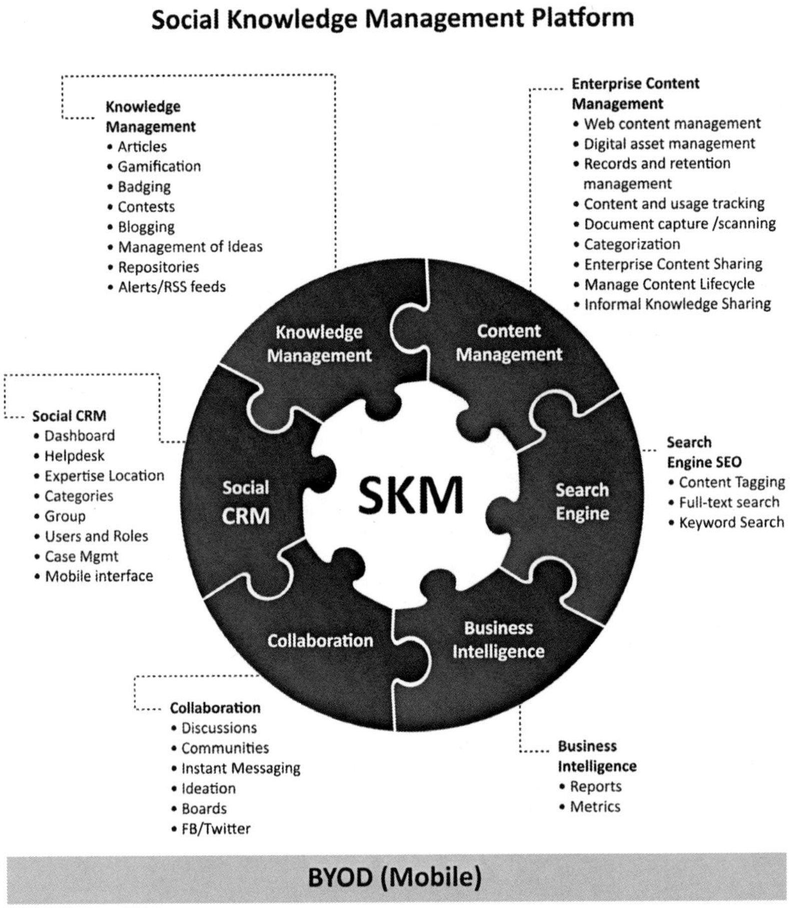

You first need to understand the workflow processes that currently exist so you can design processes around these activities. Second, understand where there are opportunities for optimization within the current processes, which will create an *enhanced human experience* for the knowledge worker. And lastly, identify where workflow integrations can be introduced that will create a seamless process, mitigating the need for the knowledge worker to *porpoise* across various capabilities to find, retain, iterate, and share content.

Even with the focus on understanding and leveraging existing processes, a social knowledge transformation within an organization is very much a culture shift and will require investment in *organization change management*, highlighted in Chapter 4. It will be a balancing act to understand the required changes, the time commitment, and the organization's tolerance and ability to absorb the changes.

This list of capabilities represents a vision of SKM that combines capabilities through seamless integrations. Before you start to engage various vendors in a dialogue about SKM capabilities, you should prioritize capabilities and identify the expected benefits that address your highest-priority business objectives. For example, if your organization's top concern is building out a community that will enable Customer Support to sync with support-related Twitter and Facebook feeds across any device (BYOD), you'll want to focus on the Social Platform vendors whose capabilities best align with that goal.

Below is an example matrix that maps organizational currencies to the capabilities of a SKM platform. This will allow you to understand what currency maps to the capability in a quick and easy way. This will help you align what capabilities need investment based on the currencies that are most important to you.

Capability/Currency Matrix

SKM Business Benefits (Currencies)

SKM Platform Capabilities	Enhanced Human Experience	Competence Acceleration	Collaboration	Content Creation Cycle	Contribution (Tracking)
Enterprise Content Management		✓		✓	✓
Social CRM (Roles, Access and Case Management)	✓		✓	✓	✓
Real-Time Social Collaboration	✓	✓	✓	✓	
Social Features (Gamification, Badging, Ideation, Boards)	✓	✓	✓	✓	
Search Engine	✓	✓		✓	
Knowledge Management		✓		✓	✓
Business Intelligence		✓		✓	✓

Below is a high-level explanation of each of the capabilities and their impact within the SKM platform:

- **Enterprise Content Management:** This will be important as you consider *publishing* content for public consumption.
    - **Impact:** Ensure branding and compliance guidelines are followed.
- **Social CRM:** Management and tracking of incidents and cases, and linkage of knowledge assets to cases via appropriate access.

  - **Impact:** User identified/tagged value linking cases and knowledge for better/faster case resolution.

- **Real-Time Social Collaboration:** Coherent social strategy that is integrated real-time into the workflow activities of the users, and tightly coupled with the knowledge management capabilities.

  - **Impact:** Increased productivity and retained corporate memory to facilitate reuse while improving customer satisfaction.

- **Social Features:** Capabilities associated with a social platform that includes discussion boards, ideation, incentive-based capabilities (gamification, badging) as well as other capabilities.

  - **Impact:** Increased overall collaboration and optimization of team interaction.

- **Search Engine:** Integrated and federated search capabilities allowing users to search from within SKM as well as search SKM from an organization's enterprise search capabilities.

  - **Impact:** Leverage value of, and access to, knowledge assets from across the enterprise.

- **Knowledge Management:** Tightly coupled integration to existing KM capabilities or the creation of new capabilities.

  - **Impact:** Ability to leverage existing knowledge assets and create new ones seamlessly within one environment.

- **Business Intelligence:** Ability to report on activities across the SKM platform.

  - **Impact:** Track value and usage of environment, showing trends to help drive investment and manage environment effectively.

Below is an example of a format that can be used to assess service providers as it relates to SKM. Based on your company uniqueness, you may choose to add additional capabilities that are important to your environment.

Vendor Assessment

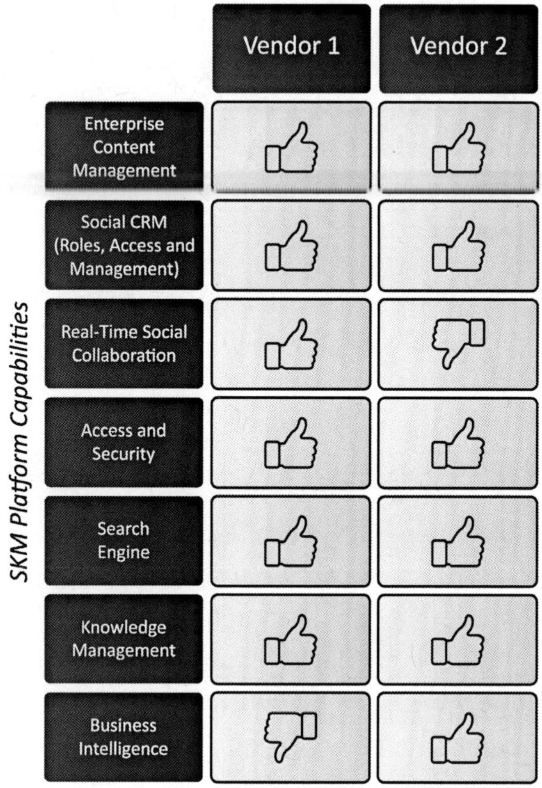

When selecting a vendor, it is best to engage a consulting partner that can help you perform an independent, platform-agnostic evaluation of all of the capability vendors in the Social Knowledge Management space.

Here is a list of capabilities that a consulting partner should have in order to help perform a robust SKM solution assessment:

- A mature practice providing SKM Practice/Managed Services to a variety of customers.

- Certification as a technical partner with one or more Social Platform vendors.
- Best practices and methods around the full SKM Project Life Cycle (PLC) engagement. The consulting partner you choose should be intimately familiar with the unique aspects of best practices around SKM deployments such as, but not limited to:
  - Designing gamification features early on in the process: gamification is one of the most challenging, yet critically important elements of Social Knowledge that helps drive adoption and usage of SKM.
  - Identifying the level of *social*: For example, do you want to open up communities that enable your product marketing team to collaborate with customers on Twitter and Facebook? Or is the project geared toward accelerating internal communication between two teams such as Technical Support and Engineering?
  - Understanding the *SKM Development Lifecycle*: Below is a view of the SKM development lifecycle that outlines key phases in a social knowledge initiative with a coupled and complementary *Content Creation Lifecycle* process.

SKM Development Lifecycle

SKM Development Lifecycle outlines the process that you can anticipate following as you deploy a Social Knowledge Management Environment (SKME):

- **SKM Needs Analysis:** Identify the business goals and objectives by interviewing leadership, managers, and subject matter experts (SMEs) relative to social knowledge. Consider current capabilities and gaps in the capabilities that enable the organization to source, retain, iterate, and share knowledge effectively.

- **SKM Requirements Definition:** Based on the business drivers (discussed earlier in this chapter), needs, and associated gap analysis, consider the best practices and SKM capabilities to develop requirements that reflect the needs of your organization.
- **SKM Vendor Assessment:** Based on your requirements, perform a vendor evaluation assessing how these vendors can meet your business requirements. Proof of Concept (PoC), or Trial-by-Fire evaluation processes, are beneficial as you are able to get an understanding of capabilities based on your requirements, rather than generic capability.
- **SKM Design**: Based on requirements and best practices, design the platform based on business drivers that are most important to your organization. Moreover, there are unique capabilities associated with SKM that must be considered to help drive adoption and usage of the platform. At this point, make sure you consider these capabilities that may not have been part of your initial requirements (e.g. gamification, badging, labels).
- **Development and Integration:** Traditional development activities that may include configuration, custom development, and integrations.
- **Stage/Test/Pilot:** Standard testing of the capabilities being delivered. Having small pilot activities is important to expose users to capabilities to identify gaps in functionality and process. This also builds a *champion*

network of users in the organizations for those that have had early exposure to the SKME.

- **Deploy:** It is not advised to approach an SKM with a "big bang" approach. It is important show early success, even if it is a small segment of the team. Given that this is as much a culture shift as it is a technology implementation, it is critical to consider the change management aspects and learning through your initial phases of your implementation. Identify a group of early adopters that would quickly realize benefit from an SKM deployment. It is important to show measurable benefit to help with the overall adoption of the SKM platform.

Content Creation Lifecycle is a complementary and critical process that should be followed to increase your chances of success when implementing an SKME:

- **Content Analysis:** This step outlines the need to assess your current content inventory, understanding what is available, what is accurate, where investments need to be made, and the general state of your knowledge assets. From this analysis, you will define what actions need to take place to get these assets to a point where they can be shared and reused.

- **Content Seeding:** There are two ways of looking at seeding content: broad and shallow or narrow and deep. Your deployment approach will help you decide the most appropriate path. If you choose to do a "big bang" deployment it will be important to have content across a broad set of categories within your SKME. Whereas if you target a specific group or product area for the initial deployment, you can go deep by investing in content within a particular area or discipline.

- **Content Migration:** Once your content is identified, and depending on the volume of content you have, the choice to either manually migrate content or invest in an automated process to move content becomes necessary. If the content is manageable, it is recommended to move content manually since it makes the user familiar with the environment as well as the capabilities required to add and modify content. It should be noted that if the authors of the content populate it with their userid, the system will pick this up as contributions and count toward their recognition and reputation (i.e. gamification and badging).

- **Content Quality Algorithm:** It will be important to develop a quality scoring mechanism that weighs the value of the content based on attributes important to your organization (i.e. likes, kudos, contributions, authors, solution linkage). This algorithm is important as it will surface knowledge assets that are valuable, based on your established criteria, and be an input for business rules that will help manage content proactively (archive, update, delete).

Below is a consolidated representation of a mature Social Knowledge Management Environment. The human experience is core to the success of a Social Knowledge Management Environment. It is important that the sharing and collaboration is seamless with the ability to search, create, iterate, and share knowledge.

Currencies and Benefits

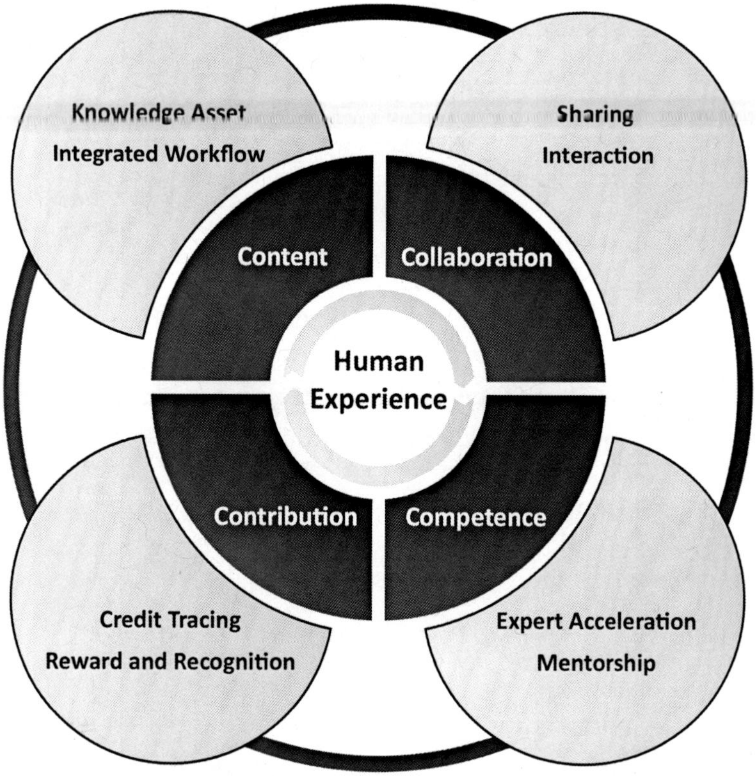

Each of the organizational currencies (Content, Collaboration, Competence, Contribution and an Enhanced Human Experience) represents real value to the organization and to the individual:

- **Content**
  - Organizational Value: Retained corporate memory that drives improved productivity across employees.
  - Individual Value: Ability to leverage knowledge to solve problems fast and better – allowing higher performance levels.
- **Collaboration**
  - Organizational Value: Integrated sharing and interacting in an environment that can retain and reuse experiences – facilitating corporate memory that would otherwise be lost.
  - Individual Value: Seamless access to experts across the enterprise to engage and glean knowledge in real-time within existing workflow.
- **Competence**
  - Organizational Value: Accelerated expertise based on access to knowledge and human experts within the environment – increasing overall productivity of the organization.
  - Individual Value: Increased performance to more quickly to meet and exceed KPI (key performance indicators).

- **Contribution**
  - Organizational Value: Creation of critical mass of knowledge assets with an associated *knowledge network* that can be understood and polled against when business needs arise in specific areas of the business.
  - Individual Value: Recognition and reputation as an expert, as well as individuals connecting and engaging with other experts.

Next, let's consider how these currencies can be measured and tracked. Organization and individual value is important, but a mature SKM practice leverages the currencies from a quantitative perspective as well. Following is a look at specific measures and accompanying metrics.

Return on Investment (ROI)/Tracking/Measures

In order to justify moving toward an SKM practice, one of the first steps is to review what measures, metrics, and tools that are currently in place within an organization. As you review this information, you may consider how they might be extended as you deliver the SKM capability.

Below is a sampling of common measures and metrics categories, and some thoughts on how they may be enhanced as you deliver an SKM solution.

Customer Marketing/Sales/Partner Function Measures

In the Marketing, Sales, and Partner functions, these are common measures used:

- Campaign tracking and channel effectiveness
- Chief Marketing Officer (CMO) dashboards, marketing contribution to revenue
- Demand funnel reporting (inquiry to close)
- Email and campaign metrics for analyzing marketing effectiveness
- Website analytics dashboards for monitoring site conversion and utilization
- Metrics around third-party business intelligence and analytics solutions

Leveraging SKM, the following marketing metrics can be extended to consider the impact of Social Knowledge Management. Below is a sampling of areas to consider:

Marketing Measures

Metrics Category	Measures (Post-SKM)
Campaign Tracking	• Qualitative Social Connections • SKM Pass-Thru (Likes)
Channel Effectiveness	• Cross-Company Contribution • Channel Pass-Thru via SKM
Marketing Pipeline Influence	• SKM Facilitated Opportunities • Forum Outreach/Participation
Email Metrics	• Email to Social Conversion • SKM Outreach Conversion
Web Analytics	• Social Traffic/Contribution • Contribution Segmentation
Solution Selling	• SKM Coordinated Selling • Knowledge Asset Creation

Customer/Technical Support Function Measures

Within the customer support realm, there are a number of metrics categories that can be influenced by SKM:

- Knowledge contribution and utilization
- Case management metrics
- Customer satisfaction, customer self-service, productivity (internal)

Leveraging SKM, the following customer support metrics can be extended to consider the impact of Social Knowledge Management. Below is a sampling of areas to consider:

Customer/Technical Support Measures

Metrics Category	Measures (Post-SKM)
Knowledge Utilization »	• SKM Views, Likes, Contribution • Content/Knowledge Creation
Case Management »	• Case Avoidance • Knowledge Linkage
Customer Satisfaction »	• SKM Facilitated Support • Support Channel Comparison
Customer Self-Service »	• Access and Utilization • Segmentation of Participation
Contributions (Internal) »	• Agent Creation and Contribution • Level of Collaboration (Badging)
Productivity (Internal) »	• Expert Acceleration • SKM Influenced Case Metrics

Dashboards are popular and effective in communicating status and value quickly. Leveraging a dashboard with a Social Knowledge Management Environment in place, you'll experience a mixture of base activity measures and metrics as well as dynamic business driven (financial) measures. Keeping your eye on ever-changing business-related information within an SKME will assist in justifying continued investments, not just within SKM, but across your organization.

SAMPLE KPIs & MBOs

SKM Scorecard View - Against Goals (Q/Q)

Financial KPIs				
Metric	Target	Q1	Q2	STATUS
Case Avoidance Cost Savings	$14M	$2.6M	$3.9M	Y

External Customer				
Metric	Target	Q1	Q2	Q3
4/5 Scale of Satisfaction	4.5	0	4.6	4.5

People Leadership				
Metric	Target	Q1	Q2	STATUS
Team # Recognition and/or Awards	4	3	1	R
Team # Speaking Engagements	10	1	3	Y
Industry Recognition # Awards	3	0	0	G

Internal Operations				
Metric	Target	Q1	Q2	STATUS
Content Quality	[illegible] of content should be rated quality			R
Content Capture	1% of total cases linked to content			Y
Content Effectiveness	2% of cases closed linked to existing content			G
Article Published	600			
External views of published content	930K Views			
Participating Customer Accounts	50			
SKM Platform Issues Tracked	25% reduction			
Communities Managed	4			
# Patents Applied	1			

When you consider an SKM deployment, you will quickly realize that you will need an entirely new set of *social* measures and accompanying metrics, so let's go a bit deeper. It is important to quantify and track how the *social* aspect of your Social Knowledge Management Environment is performing in relation to the five *Organizational Currencies* (Content, Collaboration, Contribution, Competence, and Enhance Human Experience).

- **How Social are we?** You can measure participation by developing a set of metrics that captures the level of interactions across all the of the collaboration tools. These metrics are important in tracking how much, and the level of, *Collaboration* (currency) being generated across your organization.

- **How successful is our Social content?** How successful is your social content in answering questions (case deflection, perhaps)? Is the viewing of content by user going in an upward trend? Is it staying flat? Going down? All knowledge and SKME utilization metrics should be monitored and action plans developed as appropriate as data indicate. As an example, if the number of opened cases (online or phone) is going up and viewing of content is staying flat or going down, you most likely have issues. The users may not be finding content (search), the content is not there (gap), or there may be quality issues with the content that impacts the overall *trust* factor! These observations, particularly the final element of trust, help bring understanding and quantifiable value to the *Contributions* (currency) of the members of your community.

  You should also pay attention to the specific, and possibly external, content users leverage and link to in order to complete their work (especially when closing cases, adding a new contribution). New knowledge workers leverage content regardless of original source. Your SKM Practice (and SKME) must be able to manage content and linking in order to expose the benefit associated with driving *Competence* (currency) in the organization.

- **How Successful are we at Promoting and Rewarding Social?** It is real-time recognition, kudos, likes, and two-way interactions and acknowledgements (gamification) that help endear users to an online space, and these techniques are just as important when considering SKM.

In addition, developing instant gratification mechanisms (advance to higher levels of access, responsibility, and exclusive content) can motivate sustained, active participation and contribution. Having measures and metrics that capture how many awards, badges, and promotions are given out/viewed is key to understanding the *Enhanced Human Experience* (currency).

- **How valuable is our Social Knowledge Content?** It is important to track how many knowledge assets are generated and published from dynamic interactions within your SKME. Knowing how, the volume, and the usefulness of content, the quality, are key metrics (outside of traditional KM creation measures and metrics) to understanding how valuable the *Content* (currency) is within your SKME

Below is a graphic that encapsulates a sampling of the alignment between some example measures and metrics and the five organizational currencies. Based on your organization and your business model, you will inevitably have additional measures and metrics that will be important to your organization.

Sampling of Meaningful "Social" Knowledge Management Environment Measures & Metrics

Now that we reviewed the business benefits and some key SKM measures and metrics to consider, let's review the high-level tangible ROI that comes from evaluating how an SKM solution fits within your current application footprint. In order to do that, you will need to:

- Create an architectural diagram of what systems your organization currently has deployed and what level of integration you have achieved across applications.

- Outline what business problem/requirements the applications and tools are currently addressing and where they fall short.
- Assess your current capabilities against that of the Social Knowledge Platform capabilities to identify where your current applications are falling short. This will be an important consideration when evaluating the overall ROI of moving from, or integrating, disparate business systems (such as KMS, CRM, Collaboration tools, and Search Engines) to deliver an SKM solution.

Depending upon the maturity of your current capabilities (Knowledge Management/Self-Service Support/Marketing/Partner), your organization will need to make critical decisions around which existing systems will be retained, extended, or retired when your organization moves to an SKM solution. One consideration is the option to jump-start a Social Knowledge Management Environment independent of your current application footprint with a pilot program.

Starting with a pilot implementation gives you flexibility to take SKM out for a test drive, make adjustments, and get the organization ready with a larger deployment. Deciding to go with a pilot also gives your organization more time to migrate off systems that are not serving your new social knowledge management direction.

Magnitude of Change

Organization Architecture considers an organization's tolerance for change, ability to absorb new information, and history. It addresses the structure of an organization, its governance, culture, politics, and espoused vs. in-place processes. The topic of *Organization Architecture* will be discussed in further detail in Chapter 4, but we will address it now at a high level before we consider the Magnitude of Change related to different SKM solution deployments. It's important to understand that an SKM rollout is just as much, if not more, of an organizational change impact as it is a technology shift. The knowledge worker's processes will change, motivations and incentives will change, and how they will be measured will change, if not transform, how the organization operates.

For a rudimentary discovery effort, a cursory Organization Architecture assessment can reveal specific areas of interests and possible areas for examination.

Methodology/Framework

> Knowing the tolerance for change is a critical element of organization architecture. For example, is the organization ahead of the curve, a fast follower or simply existing day to day? Being aware of an organization's past, current and aspirational state helps determine which roadmaps, patterns, templates, and best practices are appropriate.

Team (Fit, Function, and Performance)

> Does the organization have a robust approach to Intellectual Capital? Do they have the *right talent* at the *right time*? Good

planning and strategies does not always translate to good decision-making.

Success Criteria, Approach, and Vision

Is there a good understanding of what success looks like? Have specific areas such as technology stability, overall (non-punitive) governance, talent issues, and architecture frameworks been identified and targeted for improvement? A balance of innovation and action with a focus on the business needs of the technology function can help organizations transition and transform from a traditional *task shop* to a mature *innovator*. Is the organization engaged and aware of the business implications technology has on the organization's product, the market, and the bottom line (financial impact)?

Below are two graphics for your consideration that outline the impact of change relative to the benefits associated with the organizational currencies.

SKM Opportunity Focus Area
By Level of Change Magnitude + Complexity

High

Enhance Customer Experience

Enhance Partner/Channel Experience

Medium

Improve Internal Customer Support (Non Tech/Tech) Productivity

Improve Internal Sales & Marketing Productivity

Low

Enhance Internal/Corporate Collaboration Across Teams

ROI vs Change Magnitude/Complexity by Opportunity Focus Area

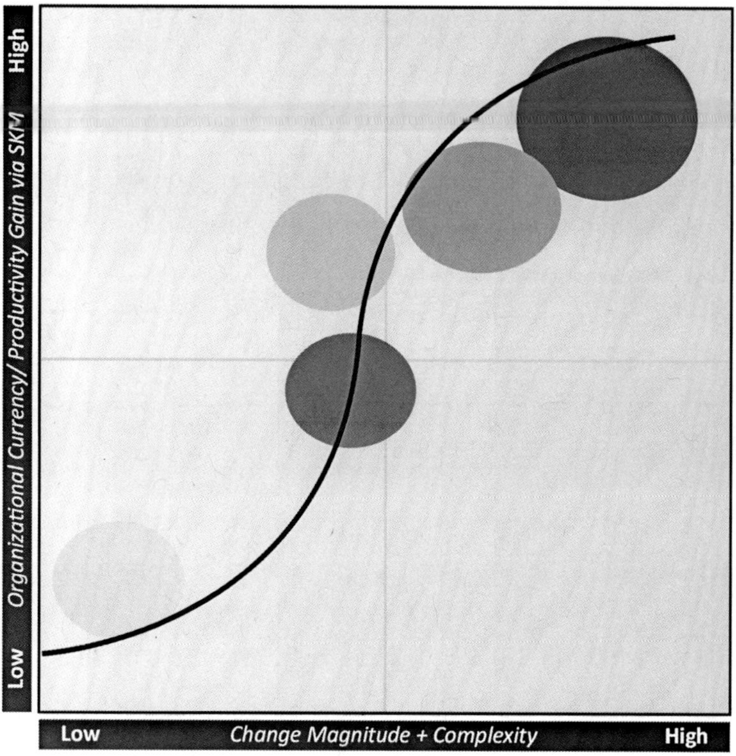

As you move to the upper right of the graphic the impact to change is greater, but the benefits related are greater, too. Moreover, the audience moves from an internal facing team, in which you have more control, to an external audience, where you have less control and must depend more on influence, creating a greater change impact. The balancing act is to identify the low-hanging fruit in your organization that will bring the greatest impact with least initial investment. Remember, the easiest group to implement may not be the group that will deliver the most benefit. It is important to have a meaningful (impactful) launch of an SKM initiative to ensure the success of future phases.

Understanding What Makes Your Organization Unique

Every organization is different. They can be large or small, flush with a mountain of cash, or just getting by. Just as all organizations are different, all frameworks, models, and approaches are different as well. Every organization, department, and team should be able to define their *culture* (what makes it unique and successful), foster, and promote it. *If your team does not have a sense of culture it will struggle with an SKM deployment.*

Below is a table that includes cultural attributes that complement, as well as, hinder the potential for a successful SKM rollout. Where your culture is represented by the *SKM Challenging Attributes*, it will be your job to mitigate those through incentives or change management efforts.

SKM Cultural Attributes

Enabling Attributes	Challenging Attributes
Dynamic	Static
Open	Closed
Trusting	Resistant
Innovative	Skeptical
Team Centered	Individualism
Collaborative	Controlling
Iterative	Linear

Before you get on the road to implementing SKM, now is the time to do what it takes to drill down on what is unique to your organization and what aspects of your organization are things you want to promote (hold an offsite!). If you are struggling without an identity, then start out by focusing on things your organization wants to *start* promoting as you turn the corner on a new way of sharing … it will be rewarding and will set the groundwork for getting ready for a successful SKM practice.

Quick List: Understand the mechanics of SKME.

How do Social Knowledge Management Environments work?

- Integration of enterprise collaboration, content management, and knowledge management in a unified process, supporting the entire knowledge asset lifecycle from end-to-end.
- Knowledge through collaboration –method/approach remains even if type of content is different.
- Meaningful knowledge is dynamically exposed within the workflow process based on attributes captured (i.e. CRM).
- Knowledge is captured dynamically within real-time workflow processes.
- Sentiment and reputation are calling cards of the content and the knowledge worker

Why do SKMEs work?

- An opportunity exists to create content dynamically in a way that supports the rapid acceleration of social knowledge workers; content that can be freely accessed, iterated, and available instantly.
- Outcomes represent tangible value to the users.
- Aligned to incentives, business processes, and workflow.
- User for user – helping themselves and others at the same time.

What do SKMEs look like when they are working?

- Crowdsourcing – accelerated access to experts
- Knowledge lifecycle origination – credit tracing, provenance, and *knowing the source*
- Collaborative environments – producing useful knowledge assets
- Knowledge assets valued and iterated - recognition

Step by Step: Want to try something today?

Follow this process:

1. Make a list of the successful (and the failed) initiatives in the organization over the past five years.
2. Note any disconnect between specific layers of management. Is everyone communicating? What challenges do they face?
3. Note the *real versus the espoused* (organizational policies, drivers for change, points of view, barriers). What is stated as a goal or important to the organization but maybe not actually carried out.
4. Identify what makes your organization unique and successful. Does your organization/department/team need to work on building a road to a positive, productive culture? Start now (!) and outline the steps you can take to develop a productive environment.

Chapter 4 – The New Road: Organization Architecture, Opportunities, and Best Practices

The value of Social Knowledge is in its *generation*. This is true in a classical use of the word, as in *to generate*, but it's also true when you think about social knowledge being aligned with a group of individuals with similar ideas, expectations, and experiences. Specifically, within a Social Knowledge Management Environment new knowledge is generated when people have conversations, build communities, and collaborate. Unfortunately, such collaboration rarely happens in a scheduled or planned way. Spontaneity is a hallmark of Social Knowledge and getting to, and capturing, meaningful knowledge actually requires a bit of finesse.

Think about when the first personal computers became commonplace and the exponential nature in which content began to be created, shared, and saved. Now, with the advent of social technologies and practices coupled with traditional technologies, the ability to leverage, share, and iterate content has reached a new stage of amplification. Social technologies have become second nature to the new millennium generation (as well as for those following in their footsteps) and the expectation is that these capabilities and proclivities will be inherent in other processes that involve sharing, learning, or contributing content. As an example, recognition and associated reputation building are key elements of gamification and other social media experiences, and should be part of your SKM strategy.

The value of providing near instantaneous validation of one's skills, contributions, and experiences translate well to traditional business environments. Social Knowledge sparks a collaborative (even competitive) element that traditional Knowledge Management efforts have lacked. The ability to work dynamically, share information quickly, and leverage enhanced dashboards conveying valuable metrics are appealing to any generation, but to those individuals with an inherent knowledge (and expectation) of collaborative technology, it's just common sense.

For an SKM effort to create a lasting and sustainable impact within an organization, it has to have maximized communication, created an agile governance structure, and delivered on the right set of tools and technology to meet the needs of the business. But as described previously, the organization must gain a better understanding of its greatest resource: *its people.*

Organization Architecture

Social Knowledge Management is transformative. Organization Architecture is a key element within any SKM effort and is necessary to facilitate the transformation. It includes dramatic changes in the experiences, techniques, and processes within an organization. SKM taps into the information flow and fosters the creation of knowledge assets that can be captured and retained as part of organizational memory. It also impacts the structure of an organization, its governance, culture, and politics. Because SKM has such a sweeping impact across the organization, it is important that Organization Architecture, and its key components, be considered.

Organization Architecture defines your organization's tolerance for change, ability to absorb new information, and history. It addresses the structure of an organization, its governance, culture, politics, and espoused as opposed to *in place* processes.

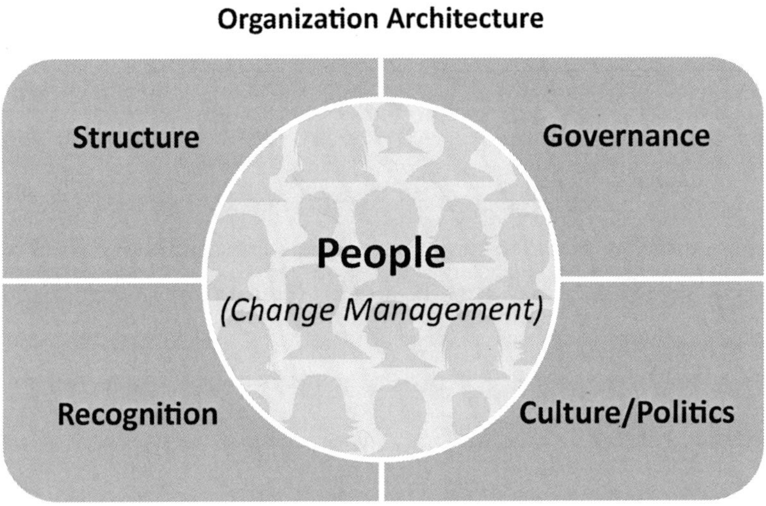

Structure

To maximize the benefits of SKM within an entity, it is critical to consider the organization structure in a way that aligns and promotes specific behaviors. We do that by looking at the *services* that are offered as part of an SKM practice.

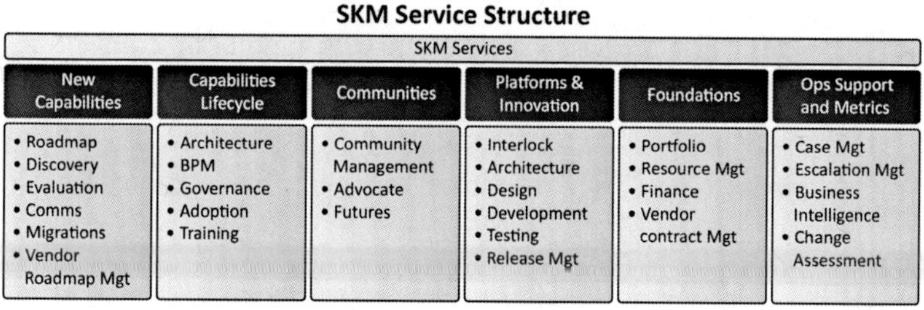

Each of these services plays a critical role in the success of an SKM Practice.

- **New Capabilities:** The role of this service area is to identify and assess opportunities for the practice to pursue. As previously mentioned, it is important to develop a strategy that identifies opportunities that have a proclivity to be *early adopters* and have business models that can gain immediate value from an SKM environment. The attributes of such opportunities include:
    - Highly interactive workflow processes
    - Activities/work effort is complex or diverse
    - Dependent on dynamic knowledge assets
    - Access to expert knowledge workers
    - Flexible to organizational change
    - Comfortable with ambiguity

  Once a new opportunity is identified, the *New Capability* service provides evaluation, communication, and roadmap services to ensure the practice is aligned. The SKM blueprint is established and activities captured, tracked, and developed within an SKM environment.

Common Roles: SKM Program Manager, SKM Project Manager, SKM Team Lead

- **Capabilities Lifecycle:** This service area oversees and is the authoritative source for the SKM practice. The overall governance and management oversight is provided to ensure opportunities are continuously managed and environments are maintained. Engagement models, as part of overarching business architecture are defined, deployed, and managed within this service area.

  Common Roles: SKM Practice Manager, SKM Program Manager, SKM Engagement Manager

- **Communities:** SKM environments, often called communities, require continual oversight. An individual or team, often called Community Manager(s), provide SKM subject matter expertise and guidance as well as advocacy for the users of the SKM environment.

  Common Roles: Community Manager, SKM Team Lead, Community Administrator, Community Moderator, Champions

- **Platform and Innovation:** This service is focused on design, development, integration, testing, deployment, and ongoing support of Social Knowledge Management technology.

Common Roles: SKM Technology Leader, SKM Engineer, SKM Developer, SKM QA Engineer, SKM Integration Engineer

- **Foundational:** Baseline services that track and manage costs, resources, vendor contracts, and other business functions to support the SKM practice activities.

  Common Roles: SKM Program Manager, SKM Team Lead

- **Operational Support and Metrics:** This service provides case and escalation management support, as well as metrics management. This facilitates support and escalation while tracking overall usage.

  Common Roles: SKM Technology Operations Manager, SKM Support Manager, SKM Business Intelligence Manager, SKM Team Lead

Governance

SKM governance guides the integration, design, construction, deployment, and management of all the SKM Practice Solutions through principles, policies, standards, and models that reflect an organization's business strategies, requirements, and constraints. It includes the following:

- Developing practices that ensure accountability to the stakeholder community.
- Implementing a system of controls over the creation and monitoring of architecture components and activities, to

ensure the effective introduction, implementation, reuse, and evolution of SKM within the organization.

- Implementing a system of record to ensure compliance with internal and external standards.

As an SKME moves from concept to pilot to maturity, a solid yet agile governance process is critical to keeping its initiative on target. The SKME program team should be encouraged to create a governing body that will make critical decisions and prioritize initiatives. The governing body plays a critical role in driving the direction of the SKME and creates an opportunity for stakeholders to have a sense of ownership. This, over time, helps the SKME have sustained and long-term adoption.

The size of the governing body can depend on the size and diversity of the user base, and the complexity of the organizational needs and resulting SKME. However, the number of contact points between the governing body and SKME owners should be kept to a minimum to avoid miscommunications.

Culture and Politics

Central to your transformative Social Knowledge Management initiative is an organization's past combined with its day-to-day operational culture. This includes impacts of office politics, conflicts, and tolerance for change. In the SKM world, *value is not measured by what you know; it is measured by what you share.* This is a tectonic shift for many:

- People conditioned to capturing and retaining knowledge for their individual purposes are not often inclined to share insights (also known as the *hoarder mentality*). Successful change depends on an individual's particular perspective and experience with regard to sharing and collaborating.

- Experts that may have been hidden in the past, suddenly come into view in the virtual world. How will they react? Will they view it as a positive or a negative?
- New knowledge workers and seasoned knowledge workers have equal access to information. This can be seen as a loss of competitive advantage by some workers and they may feel threatened.
- The new generation of knowledge workers may be discounted by the incumbent generation. SKM levels the playing field, enabling an interactive bi-directional knowledge channel for all.

Each of these, and others, represent dramatic changes for individuals and groups that must be considered and addressed while pursuing an SKM initiative. To help facilitate change, incentive and recognition programs, which are crucial tools in the success of any Social Knowledge effort, must be assessed, designed, and deployed. Below are a few techniques to help optimize your organization's SKM journey.

Recognition

Central to the success and adoption of any Social Knowledge Management Environment is the ability to recognize, incent, and reward behaviors that help deliver on the promise of Social

Knowledge. Creating incentive programs that provide ranking and badging of users, as well as introduction of gamification techniques (application of typical elements of game playing including: point scoring, points as currency, competition with others, rules of play, missions, and other activities) into the environment are crucial in driving adoption and specific behaviors.

People (Change Management)

As we discussed in Chapter 3, it is important to understand that an SKM rollout is just as much, if not more, of an organizational change impact as it is a technology shift. The knowledge worker's processes will change, motivations and incentives will change, how they will be measured will change, and that will transform how the organization operates.

We touched on the process of evaluating a proposed initiative within an Organization Architecture Change Magnitude Framework: Is it a customer-facing initiative with a big scope, impacting customers, partners and customer support? Or, is it an internal-only initiative with a limited scope of resources, but entails a high degree of process change?

In this section, we will review what Change Management activities exist during the lifecycle of your initiative. We will focus on the first big Change Management deliverable that must be completed for any project this transformational: The Change Magnitude Assessment.

It is critical, before you start your project or attempt to get Stakeholder/Executive buy-in, to develop the Change Magnitude

Assessment. As a first step, line up all of the Change Management activities and deliverables to ensure your project's success. Get your Change Management toolbox ready!

Below is a sample list of Change Management deliverables/activities by project phase:

Scoping and Change Impact Review:

Sponsor and Role Definition

Change Management Status Report

Change Magnitude Assessment

High-Level Change Process Impact

High-Level Community/Social Training Needs Assessment

Business Stakeholder Project Commit

Change Management Resource Plan

Change Strategy and Risk Management Plan

Stakeholder Matrix/Analysis

Community Analysis and Initial Change Communication Review

High-Level Communication Plan

High-Level Training Plan

- High-Level Engagement Plan
- Business and Social KPI Metrics Review

Execute Commit

- Detailed Stakeholder Engagement Plan
- Community –based 360 Workflow Review
- Full Business Impact Analysis and Risk Mitigation Summary
- Communication Plan
- Change Success Metrics (included in Business KPI metrics)
- Community Readiness Plan

Operational Readiness Review

- Communication Materials
- Training Content and Delivery Plan
- Business Readiness Assessment Report
- Training Metrics
- Final Community Adoption Assessment
- Risk Mitigation Readiness Plan

Implementation & Post Go-Live Transition

Post Implementation Transition Plan

SKME Community Support Plan

Project Close Communication

Post Project Assessment

Executive Summary (includes Change Adoption Metrics)

Organization Change Management has to be an important part of any transformational project. It must have the appropriate resources and time allocated to ensuring all the deliverables are met and the change adoption engine is started at the very early stages of the project lifecycle.

The most important early deliverable, as discussed above, is the Change Magnitude Assessment. This is the first real, hard look at what the true change impact is going to be within your organization. Here is an overview of what a Change Magnitude Assessment covers:

Organization Change Magnitude Assessment Overview

- Designed to Understand the Complexity and Business Impact at a High Level
- Document Assessments about the SKM Initiative
- Gets Everyone on the Same Page About What is Needed to Enable the Business
- Usually Completed at Start of a Project or When Assessing an SKM initiative
- Includes Business Impact Questions with Score Rating from 1 (Low) to 5 (High)
- Total Score Determines the Change Magnitude of Low to High

Organization Change Magnitude Assessment
Sample Questions/Scoring

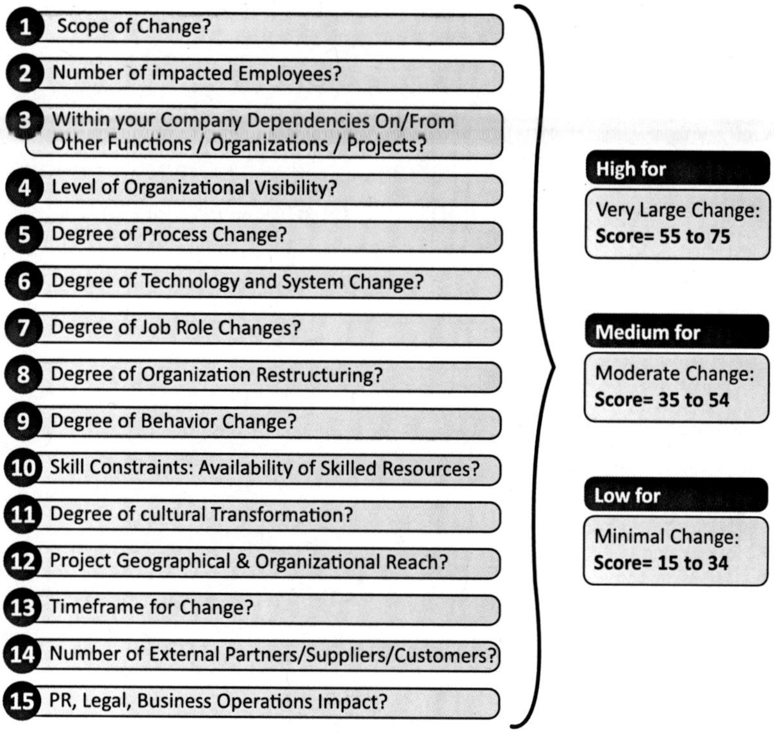

The Organization Change Magnitude Assessment is the first Change Management deliverable, but it is important to point out that all of the tools in the Change Management toolbox are critical as you progress through each SKM project phase.

The Human Experience (Change Adoption) as it relates to SKM is crucial to consider. One of the key factors involved in delivering a successful SKME is starting out with a keen understanding of the history and results of past projects, the culture and stakeholders.

The impacts of the past will provide insights and point to pathways for future successes. Moreover, benchmarking success and best practices from outside your organization will be important to ensure correct baselines and success metrics are established. Remember, it is the people (and their participation) that drive the success or failure of an SKM initiative. Please go to our website at www.socialknowledgemanagement.com to obtain more samples of Change Management checklists and deliverables.

Capability and Opportunities

As you consider the Organization Architecture elements in preparation for a successful SKM journey, SKM exposes a new opportunity to capture and make knowledge available from across the organization. SKM provides a host of robust capabilities to support your combined enterprise collaboration, knowledge management, and content management. As described in detail in Chapter 3, the core capabilities (social knowledge organizational currencies) provided by an SKME are:

Currencies and Benefits

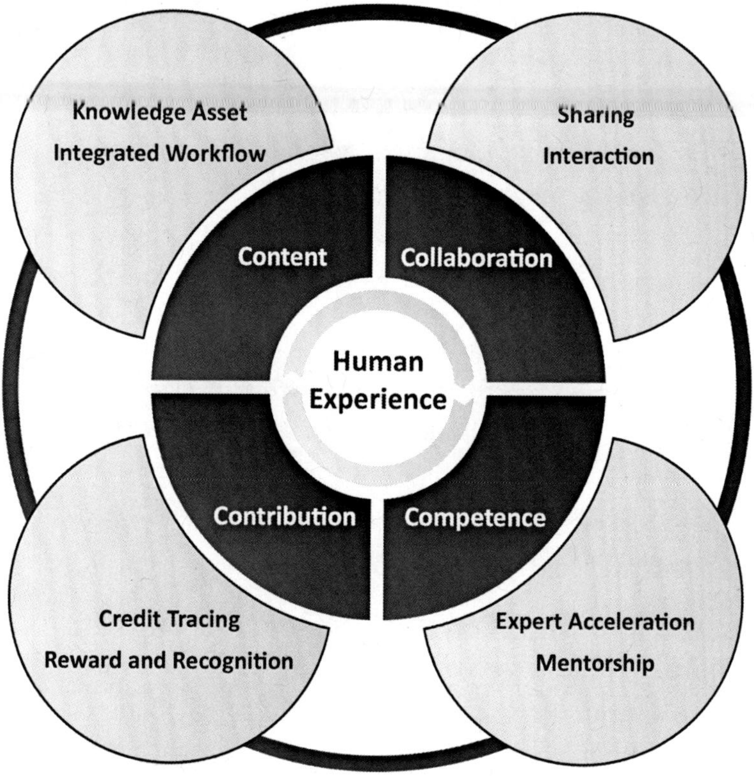

- **Content (Knowledge Assets)**: Conversations between knowledge workers are captured as content in the Social Knowledge Management environment. Everyone with access to the environment is empowered to contribute, refine, and enhance the knowledge and morph discussions into more formal knowledge assets.

- **Collaboration (Engagement/Sharing)**: Social Knowledge Management connects people and captures their conversations as they collaborate to solve business challenges.
- **Competence (Expert Acceleration)**: By enabling a Social Knowledge Management Environment, new knowledge workers will consume and absorb existing knowledge assets created by experts. Moreover, they will have the ability to easily engage experts associated with the content all within the SKME.
- **Contribution (Credit Tracing)**: Many teams experience challenges in identifying who created knowledge, where it exists within their organization, and who has contributed to it during its lifecycle. Social Knowledge Management provides the ability to do knowledge trace back (contribution tracking).
- **Enhanced Human Experience (User Experience)**: Social Knowledge Management (SKM) provides an *Enhanced Human Experience* in the form of seamless integration across and between the important capabilities that result in increased productivity and superior customer services and support. If the solution you are envisioning does not inspire and invite people to participate, create, and socialize, it will not be successful. No matter the number of incentives and KPIs put into place, if the capability is not one that is seamless to the user workflow or inherent to their natural activities, it will be hard pressed to be successful.

SKM breaks down the barriers within the organization about who can contribute and when. Beyond the core capabilities described above, the following list of opportunities broadens the scope and potential audience of the Social Knowledge Management Environment. The first in a host of opportunities SKM delivers is:

Opportunity 1 - Eliminate Knowledge Guarding: *Knowledge Guarding* is when some incumbent resources do not actively contribute to organizational knowledge. This is mitigated with the deployment of a Social Knowledge Management Environment as all resources and their contributions will be apparent.

The open collaboration capabilities give all users the ability to engage dynamically and solve real-world issues in real time. These collaborative activities include valued information (i.e. troubleshooting tactics, associated content, solutions, etc.) that can be reused, evolved into formalized knowledge assets, and much more. SKM collaboration is used across the organization by the newest, as well as the most experienced knowledge workers, which enables all resources to contribute to the corporate memory of the organization. Some of the actions and results that can be expected as knowledge guarding are eliminated:

- Increased participation by new knowledge workers
- Broader expert influence across larger virtual audience
- Reuse of knowledge assets improving productivity
- New opportunities for experts to advance and find more fulfilling ways to contribute to the organization

Opportunity 2 – Scalable Mentoring Models: New SKM experts and experienced knowledge workers will be present in the same dynamic environment. This presents an opportunity to implement and scale a new kind of *one to many* or *many to many* mentoring model.

Establish or enhance your mentoring programs to take full advantage of the capabilities of an SKM environment. Develop and establish performance indicators to support desired behavior and track the interactions within the SKM environment. Some of the actions and results that could be expected if the mentoring opportunity is pursued:

- Accelerate learning and reduced learning curve for new employees.
- New opportunities to track, then recognize, knowledge workers for specific desired behaviors.
- Ability to develop an expert knowledge worker network to engage in new projects and initiatives.

Opportunity 3 – Reward and Recognition Model: Often current Key Performance Indicators (KPIs) are defined to motivate individual learning. With the introduction of SKM, the level of collaboration and *what is shared* becomes the most highly desired KPI.

The SKM environment allows you to track the volume of contributions, views, likes/kudos, publications, and much more. These indicators track the level of collaboration within the SKME. Knowledge workers can then be acknowledged within their teams and rewarded for being an SKM champion, becoming an example to their teammates. Some of the actions and results that can be expected if a new reward and recognition model is pursued:

- Define and deliver real-time recognition and reputation model
- Establish, approve, and communicate new KPIs
- Develop and deliver knowledge reporting

Opportunity 4 – Virtual Team Formation and Development: With SKM it is no longer difficult to collaborate effectively and measure team interactions. Also, creating *crowd-curated* knowledge-sharing environments allows users to share contextually and timely relevant content.

SKME supports virtual teaming with appropriate roles, badges, and gamification for individuals and teams. The organization has the ability, via SKME, to create virtual teams organically via any number of common attributes associated with individuals or groups. Some of the actions and results that could be expected if this opportunity is pursued:

- Ability to measure and support the contributions of the individual and teams, relative to other individuals and teams.
- Spontaneous teams dynamically created across remote distances and experience levels.
- Establish teams and drive behaviors based on changing business needs.

- Build enthusiasm for initiatives and accelerate participation as teams encourage and support each other.

Opportunity 5 – Automated Content Quality Measures: Typically, content ratings are often limited to one attribute (rating or likes or kudos) that determine its usefulness. SKM allows you the potential to combine multiple attributes that include rating and likes and kudos, as well as any other attribute (solution linkage, views, and author) associated with the asset to measure usefulness of knowledge assets.

A content quality weighting formula can be applied to an asset based on a diverse set of business rules, defined by the organization, that measure the value/quality of content and its contributions to organizational success. Automated quality indexing of assets based on a quality algorithm can be used to trigger business rules that will archive, delete, or increase visibility based on specific content's quality score. Some of the actions and results that could be expected if this opportunity is pursued:

- Definition of business rules for a weighted quality equation (algorithm).
- Develop appropriate reporting metrics and leveraging results of the algorithm.
- Ability to maintain and adjust quality equation to meet changing needs.

Opportunity 6 – Everybody Supports Sales: Traditionally, limited company resources (Sales Reps, Sales Engineers, Product Managers, and Executives) are directly tasked with supporting the sales process in an organization. SKME enables a much broader community to support the sales process in a contextually sensitive way. Some of the actions and results that could be expected if this opportunity is pursued:

- Develop a sales engagement model within the SKME.
- Create measures based on user/roles, to measure sales influence.
- Tag content appropriate for audience.

Best Practices

Below are a set of best practices that will contribute to a successful launch and deliver sustained benefits of your Social Knowledge Management practice. It will be important to continue to evaluate and tweak your SKME to meet the needs of your community. Below are some ideas that will help guide your continued investment:

- **Integrated Collaborative Workflow:** To benefit from the spontaneity of the collaboration taking place within the enterprise, the SKME should be integrated with existing collaborative tools and workflow processes. Collaborative tools that exist as stand-alone tools, make it difficult to capture valuable interactions as knowledge workers skip from various tools, often leaving valuable content in disconnected areas. This inhibits the ability to effectively capture and reuse content. It also inhibits wide-spread use by making it difficult for knowledge works to collaborate within a seamless workflow. Example integrations within your SKME:

- **Integrated Knowledge and Content Management:** The SKME should have a light-weight Content Management and Knowledge Management integration to process flagged articles and assets for publication. This will enable seamless evolution of knowledge assets.
- **Integrated CRM**: Integrate SKME into Customer Relationship Management in which users of CRM will automatically be exposed to applicable knowledge assets based on the attributes of the case. This bi-directional integration with CRM is crucial to drive usage and adoption.

- **Roles and Responsibilities:** To create buy-in and adoption across the organization, it is important to idenitfy and offer roles to the knowledge worker community to participate and engage at a more in-depth level.
  - **Community Manager:** Provide daily oversight and planning activities relative to the SKME. Empower them to make and drive operational decisions, including minor configuration and SKME structure changes.
  - **Knowledge Champions:** This key role is to focus on the content and the value it represents. Having a specific role that has responsibility to help maintain and maximize the value of

the content is important to identify within the knowledge worker pool of the SKME. Tools are provided within the SKME to help teams identify which individuals, through their actions, are great candidates for this role.

- **Moderator:** They are a super user who helps other knowledge workers make the best use of SKME, but will also enforce and guide users to follow the rules and code of conduct for participating in the SKME. They also provide encouragement and have great insights for users and they are a reliable source for ideas for identifying new features and improvements/enhancements to the SKME.
- **Business Champion:** This specific role is accountable and responsible for the user community and ensuring user-centered capabilities are delivered for a successful SKME. This role works closely with the program and development team to prioritize and test (User Acceptance Testing) new capabilities and functionalities delivered.

- **Gamification and Reputation Management:** Engagement and adoption of SKME is dependent on an understanding of who and how content is contributed. It's important to recognize the knowledge workers in the form of incentives, rewards, badges, and points to help drive the intended behavior. Knowledge workers who are objectively rewarded for their contributions will express loyalty and ownership for the platform through their actions. They will compete with others to try to bring out the best in everyone and draw more knowledge users to the platform. Incentivizing users for performing positive actions within your SKME will promote usage and overall adoption across the organization.

- **Audience and Implemenation:** Initially, target groups for the first implementation, Pilot, or Proof of Concept, of the SKM are those who have the greatest potential to benefit from a Social Knowledge Management environment. Choosing the first group is critical to ensuring future wide-spread adoption. Consider the following critieria when choosing the first group to launch a new SKME:
    - Highly interactive teams
    - Varying levels of expertise in the group
    - Need to share expertise across team members
    - Content sharing is core to their existing work activities
    - Knowledge creation driven team

  Note: The first group may not be the easiest group. It is important to identify and select a group that would be dramatically impacted by the benefits of an SKME implementation.

- **Establish Guidelines:** Create a set of user guidelines that set out the usage policy for the SKME. It should include specifically what the site is and just as important, what it is not. Guidelines should be set to identify how the site should be used and actions/activities that are not suitable. You should also be prepared to outline the consequences for violating any user participation agreements.

- **Content Seeding:** With a new environment, it is important to launch with some existing content that users can view, share, and iterate. It should be richly populated in a few key areas to give a robust context to the content. Distributing small bits of content in various areas won't be enough, so try not to be tempted to establish an initial environment that is too broad. Users may find themselves in a virtual SKME *ghost town*, not wanting to be the first to contribute, post, or comment. Leverage subject matter experts to jump in early and *seed* the environment with appropriate discussions, articles, and knowledge assets that match the needs/interests of the early adopter community. *Community Managers* and *Moderators* should take on the responsibility to create a lively SKME environment by promoting discussions and engaging experts where appropriate. This will not only foster the value of the content, but also the collaborative nature of the environment. You should expect to have the community manager and moderator activity involved in promoting and engaging in the site for 60 to 90 days to *rev-up* participation.

- **Goals/Objectives:** Establish Social Knowledge KPIs to help drive adoption. KPIs are one tool you have to help promote the participation and adoption of your

SKME environment. Be careful not to depend only on KPIs to drive adoption; the human experience is the critical element that will ultimately drive the adoption of SKME. The creation of KPIs across the organization is not a small undertaking. It often requires involvement by Human Resources (HR) and management to establish and agree on the measures that will be tracked. It will be important for you to develop and engage the appropriate individuals and groups early to create an effective set of goals/objectives that can be adopted by the organization.

- **Incentive/Recognition/Gamification**: Establish reward and recognition programs integrated within the SKME providing real-time recognition; and establish team and individual incentives when milestones are reached. This is particularly important for users that traffic the site heavily – they should be recognized differently so they can act as *resident* experts that help guide other users. Resident experts address and deflect what would otherwise be a potential support requests to the organization.

Within the SKME, users are able to monitor their own progress and see how they are doing against their peers. Make sure to celebrate successes by highlighting that in prominent ways on the site with champion boards, badges, and unlocking special privileges (special access). You should at minimum acknowledge key contributors that *repeatedly* add content, respond to discussions, and flag flawed content and identify content for external consumption.

- **Robust Search Tool Integration:** Federated enterprise search (simultaneous search of multiple searchable resources) integration is critical to surface content from within SKMEs as well as other repositories (intranet, document repositories, etc.) from across the enterprise.

- **Participation/Ownership:** Engage business owners early, often, and continually from the point of initial implementation to ongoing support. It is important to have business involvement at all levels to set the correct priorities and ongoing investments.

- **Robust Business Value Metrics:** Community/social activity metrics are important to measure usage; yet it is critical to the business that value metrics such as costs, productivity, and customer satisfaction are also effectively measured. As part of the success criteria for an SKME, it is important to measure *activity*, but just as important is to measure the impact it is having on the business (e.g. case reduction, time to resolution, ROI, etc.).

Quick List: How prepared is your organization for the new road ahead?

To determine if your organization is ready for SKM:

- Review your organizational structure as compared to the SKM organizational service structure (provided in this chapter). Are there gaps and, if so, what are they?

- Review the opportunities and assess those that would most greatly benefit from an SKME to identify groups for a pilot or Proof of Concept.

- Review and identify best practices that apply to your organization.
- Review and apply the assessment guides and scorecards provided at www.socialknowledgemanagement.com.

Step by Step: Want to try something today?

Follow this process:

1. Notice when you can inject *human* capital (collaboration) into existing work flows.
2. Identify where Collaboration (Engagement/Sharing) and the need for Content (Knowledge Asset) intersect; and if it would be beneficial to track back to the source of the Contribution (Credit Tracing).
3. Look for areas where you can make a dramatic impact quickly to *prove* a concept or approach, remember it may not be the lowest hanging fruit that is the best to pursue initially.

Chapter 5 – Merging into Traffic: Trusting the Rules of the Road in the New Social Economy

As we've stated earlier, Social Knowledge begins with the conversation. Remember: *Conversations build Communities.* Going a bit deeper, companies considering a Social Knowledge Management effort should pay special attention to other *traffic* within the organization to determine the impact of the effort on the rest of the organization, as well as the impact on the expectations of a particular community. With so many initiatives competing for attention, traffic jams can be common, with the organizational will ebbing and flowing within a given organization.

As popular Social Knowledge tools and mobile applications have proliferated in the market over the last several years, the change in the way we work has accelerated. The knowledge workforce, once dominated by the Baby Boomer generation is now impacted heavily by Millennials and Generation Z. They all come to the workplace with vastly different expectations on how to work, when to work, where to work, and with whom to work.

A Generational Shift

Millennials (and even younger Gen Z workers) expect technology and collaborative interaction to be a fundamental part of their job, while older workers may be more comfortable with traditional communication tools rather than learning new ways of working. Moreover, the older workers may even discount social capabilities and activities as *not working*. To some degree, Gen Xers expect these to be part of the job as well, particularly those already in some sort of digital workforce.

Generational challenges include a total transforming workforce, and not just the *older* vs. the *younger*. There are also variations of technology agility, expectations, and arrogance within generations. Two examples are: the stigma of *job hopping* has evolved into *portability of workers* and the meaning of cultural diversity continues to change as technology makes communication instantaneous and without *filters*.

Also, generational gaps can occur when attempting to communicate. Finding ways to convey or interpret tone in the written word can be difficult. For example, eliminating idioms that don't translate well into another language or culture will help make your content more understandable by all parties.

The world is getting smaller with global events and technology bringing us closer together. An example is watching news events unfold on Twitter, like uprisings in Egypt and the Malaysia airline plane disappearance, and hearing news on social sites first before it hits the traditional news sources. Other examples are being able to stay in touch with family and friends across the world instantly, and connecting the workforce across time zones.

The Emerging Social (Knowledge) Economy

We are facing enormous societal and economic pressures and how we deal with them will depend heavily on our ability to gather, store, analyze and model large and disparate amounts of data. The interesting thing about all of this is that many organizations have accumulated mountains of data from different sources but have difficulty figuring out what to do with it or how to draw any insight (or the message/story) from it all. Financial service and large biotech organizations have a leg up on this type of thing due to their history and experience with large transactional data sets, but driving the activities surrounding this data requires a focus at the *intersection*, what we've labeled the "Kinetic Crossroads."

"Kinetic Crossroads"

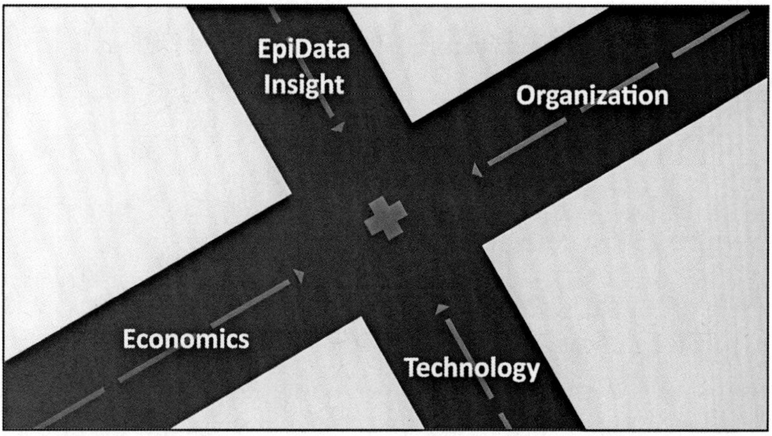

Below are the key elements that represent the "Kinetic Crossroads":

- Economic Models includes global or local impacts, market models, and complexity.
- EpiData Insight includes dynamic data, impact of environment on data expression, and value from disparate data sets.
- Organizational Change includes organizational structures, transformation, geo-political changes, and leadership.
- Technology includes high-performance computing, smart controls and processes, and nanotechnology.

Our capabilities around high-performance computing and integrated processes finally are beginning to intersect with evolving trends in data management and insight, organizational changes, and global economic and geopolitical impacts. A technology enabled, forward-thinking, and collaborative organization will be able to take advantage of this convergence and create new business models and opportunities.

What Has Worked? Where to Start?

Forward thinking organizations may want to consider how new Social Knowledge Management Environments (SKMEs) emerge and how they are quickly beginning to transform the way employees and customers create, consume, iterate, and reuse knowledge across an enterprise. Through collaboration with platform specialists such as Lithium, Salesforce, and Jive, organizations (and their clients) can jointly address innovative opportunities and challenges. Leveraging new technology methods including cloud-based delivery and dynamic data, organizations and their customers can capture, transform, and evolve intellectual capital across boundaries (real and manufactured) into knowledge assets, while keeping stakeholders informed at all stages of the process with real-time collaborative articles and communication.

Capturing and transforming institutional knowledge can occur by not only changing business processes and outcomes, but also by changing the way people think about social knowledge and collaboration. Users can collaborate to solve problems and quickly identify solutions as knowledge assets. An evolving workflow helps as well, integrating content and knowledge management dynamically. Processes are transformed and talent throughout the organization feels free (and confident) to create and collaborate with each other in such a way that others can reuse and improve upon it later.

We must push the limits and nature of collaboration, not only to extend and grow our capabilities by providing a comprehensive view of our team activities to various stakeholders, but also to promote knowledge sharing and a foundational approach to extend the thinking of new groups looking to use SKM. It is about the dynamic, collective nature of social collaboration coupled with knowledge management that signifies the value of the activities; the producing, retaining, iterating, and reusing our intellectual capital in *innovative ways.*

So what's different? People are *connecting* who hadn't been connected before and are *removing barriers* to cross-functional and cross-industry *knowledge through collaboration.* It's about leveraging business processes and workflow and establishing integral relationships with our technology that impacts the value of social knowledge collaboration.

Organizations are creating entirely new models that are showcased in everyday business processes that can be leveraged within any business function. Given the dynamic nature of collaboration, experts can be connected with users anywhere and anytime, where before they would have never known others existed. Moreover, an expert can provide mentoring and coaching to many virtually, rather than one or two in person.

It all starts with conversations, which leads to communities, which in turn leads to relevant connections. As word spreads, more people hear about it and want to be involved. A Social Knowledge Management Environment grows naturally and organically. This produces reusable knowledge, in part, because of the ownership, participation, and passion community members have in making it a success. By measuring, for example, the number of accepted solutions to questions, the activity of discussions and knowledge bases, and the overall user activity within the social knowledge management environment, it is possible to improve customer satisfaction and employee effectiveness.

A Social Knowledge Management success story is probable if your organization has two or more of the elements shown in the graphic below.

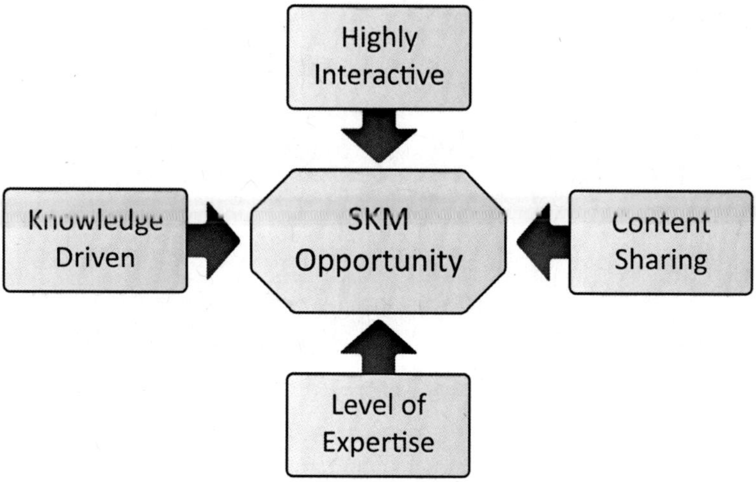

Let's review the elements that represent an SKM opportunity here:

- **Highly Interactive:** The resources in your organization actively work together to address issues, solve problems, and create new ideas. *There is an opportunity for SKM if you are struggling with the ability to capture value from collaborative activities.*

- **Levels of Expertise:** There are various pockets or degrees of expertise that can be drawn upon to help others that may have less experience in a given discipline or topic area. *There is an opportunity for SKM if your experts in the organization do not optimally contribute to the growth of others or share their knowledge effectively.*
- **Content Sharing:** Materials are shared among resources that represent "reusable assets." *There is an opportunity for SKM if this material could benefit from iterative updates from daily operational activities to stay current or if much of your content tends to be obsolete soon after it is published.*
- **Knowledge Driven:** The individual and team's performance is based on and dependent upon knowledge. *There is an opportunity for SKM if complexity inhibits the individual ability to scale to an expert quickly across multiple disciplines.*

Quick List: How do you know it is time for the Social Knowledge path in your organization?

You know it is time for Social Knowledge when:

- You can't afford to lose any more knowledge.
- You are trying to change your processes.
- You must become more transparent.
- Too many things get lost in email.
- You want to cut down on noise.
- It's time to encourage collaboration instead of hoarding.

Step by Step: Want to try something today?

Follow this process:

1. Set your goal. What do you want to accomplish?
2. Articulate the benefits. How will you sell it to your team/company?
3. Define what success looks like. How will you decide if you're successful and how much time can you give the project to succeed?
4. Relate to History. Has this (or something similar) been done before? Was it successful? Know the *environment*, the *history*, and the *culture* going into any initiative.

Chapter 6 – Express Lane: Maximizing Your Social Knowledge Potential and Knowing What is Around the Bend

We are living and working in a time of dramatic change. Our collective collaborative journeys over the last decade have forever changed how most of us interact with, leverage, and consume technology. Our expectations of technology have changed as well; we just expect it *to work*! In coming years, Social Knowledge and Social Knowledge Management will drive even more dramatic change in our lives and at work. Our knowledge economy continues to grow and as we learn how to operate as organizations enabled by Social Knowledge, our roles will evolve for everyone - including how we all interact, behave, and think.

Making the Most of Your SKM Journey

This chapter is segmented into two areas: One provides guidance on how you can take your Social Knowledge efforts to the next level and the other provides a look into the future. First, let's start with some techniques that can be employed that will help to maximize the benefits of your Social Knowledge efforts. Areas to consider include:

- **Growing Adoption:** It is a fair bet that organizational leaders want to maximize the value of the knowledge gleaned from their organizations. To increase overall value first requires understanding barriers that often are present within a Social Knowledge Management Environment, and once understood, to overcome them. Consider the bell curve below that represents two aspects of adoption: Knowledge Utilization and Knowledge Contribution. Users with less experience in the organization are more likely to use knowledge and less likely to contribute. More experienced individuals, however, will be more likely to contribute knowledge and generate knowledge assets. The challenge is to expand (widen) the bell curve so that more are using and contributing knowledge. We call the section of the curve where many are both *contributing to and drawing from* a SKME the area of *optimal adoption.*

SKM Bell Curve

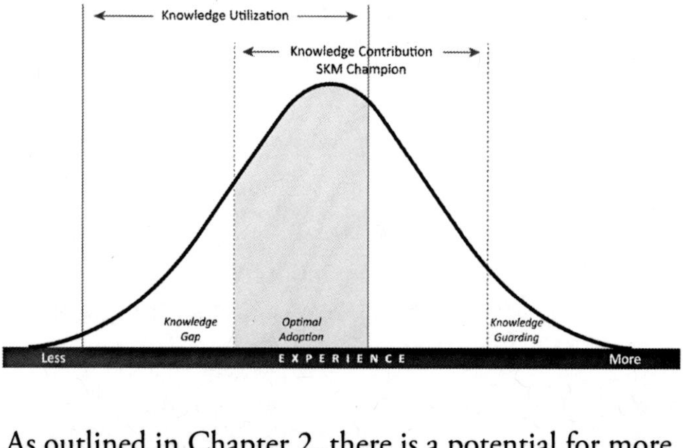

As outlined in Chapter 2, there is a potential for more experienced resources to *guard* knowledge since having knowledge has traditionally been considered a valued commodity, a badge of honor. In today's knowledge economy, the badge is earned when knowledge is shared. It becomes crucial to the success of an SKME that experienced resources are incented and rewarded for sharing knowledge assets with the entire community of users. Techniques for sharing are often in the form of gamification and reputation management capabilities. These capabilities provide a mechanism where contributors' activities are measured consistently, relative to other contributors.

Also consider the *Knowledge Gap* in which less experienced resources are hesitant to create or contribute content. As you develop an incentive program, it is important to consider inducements that will unlock the fresh perspectives within newer, less experienced individuals.

- **SKM Knowledge Network:** The content and discussions created within an SKME are ranked and rated, and provenance is tracked. You are now able to pursue and develop a robust *Knowledge Network* based on contributions, ratings, and content topics that provide a directory of expertise across the enterprise. Social Knowledge is not just about content, it is also about the social interactions and the people that are contributing. With SKM you can connect content and surface experts that may otherwise be hidden from view. Within SKM, the iteration of the knowledge asset is just as important as the initial contribution or the final result.

Below is a graphic that represents broad behaviors that are evident within an SKME. The quadrants are segmented by the proactive nature of individuals as well as their tendency to contribute content (including whether content is original or if it extends or complements another knowledge asset). The greatest opportunities for organizations are where experts are exposed through reactive contributions - lower right quadrant. Those individuals may not be actively creating content as *authors*, but they actively contribute once content has been initially created.

SKM Quadrants

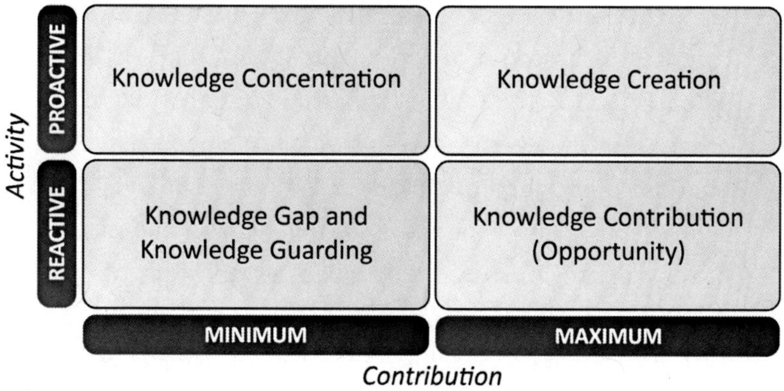

Think about people that you know that have been *published.* We generally accept authors have earned their stripes and are recognized as experts. Yet, there may be even more people that may be just as knowledgeable, but have simply chosen not to publish or perhaps haven't yet had the opportunity. A similar thing occurs in the enterprise. There are those that will author knowledge and those that have knowledge but choose not to author content. SKM makes it easier to expose and promote knowledge (including reclusive experts) for their reactive contributions.

The upper right quadrant is where knowledge assets are created and is similar to what we've traditionally called *publishing*. The upper left quadrant represents those individuals that have a very specialized area of expertise. Lastly, the lower left quadrant is an area in which you may have closely held or protected information or knowledge. We refer to this as Knowledge Guarding (Chapter 2) or a *Knowledge Gap* type of behavior, as described earlier.

- **Value of Knowledge:** Using content quality measures that can weigh a broad set of content attributes, the SKME is able to quantify the value of content based on predefined criteria. Both the social and knowledge elements can be considered and incorporated into a robust content quality algorithm to deliver the most accurate view of the value of the content. As shown below in the graphic, attributes driving the quality factor may vary from likes, views, authors, contributors, solution linkage, source and age.

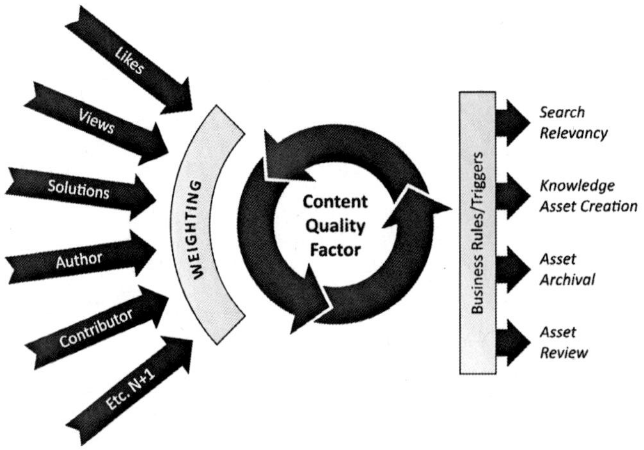

The attributes may be weighted based on the relative impact to quality. Once a Content Quality Factor is generated, it can be applied to business rules that can automatically:

- Promote valuable content by driving relevance scoring in searches.
- Trigger a business process to take action to further invest in the content.
- Archive content with low relative value.
- Any other number of actions based on the specific business needs.

- **SKM Morphing CRM:** The purpose of CRM is to address and manage customer issues and requests. The *real work* to resolve issues and support customers comes through the ability to collaborate and leverage knowledge assets. Where SKM may be a small element (or even an afterthought) to CRM today, SKM will take on a more dominant role in the organization in the future. This will become more evident as more self-service and collaborative content capabilities are provided in which customers and partners are able to address their challenges on their own – and CRM will evolve from relationship management to a repository acting more as a *Customer "Records" Management* system.

- **Extending Access:** Depending on the scope of the organizational responsibility, the SKME can be extended to provide access to partner communities in which knowledge can be shared and captured by an even broader audience. Access rights and role management become key considerations as you begin to expose an SKME to outside teams. As you consider extending access beyond your organizational boundaries, consider *Coupled Environments* below since access management will become a critical element to consider.

- **Integrating Publishing:** Exposing content beyond the SKME environment requires integration with content and knowledge management mechanisms that publish content external to SKME. This gives the ability to share content beyond users of SKME, and even expose knowledge that was spawned within the SKME to partners and customers outside of SKME. Virtual teams evolve from solving team challenges to solving organization and cross-enterprise challenges.

- **Scalable Mentoring Model:** Provides an opportunity to create virtual mentoring capabilities from what has been a one-to-one model, to a one-to-many model. Moreover, users have exposure not only to many potential mentors, but also to existing knowledge within the SKME.

SKME-Enabled Mentor Model
One-to-Many and Many-to-One

It is more than just a one-to-many mentoring model; users also have access to many resources (knowledge search, tools, existing questions, insights, guidance) contextually beyond individual experts within the Social Knowledge Management Environment. This enhances the *Expert Acceleration* benefit of SKM. Rather than just leveraging knowledge to drive expertise acceleration, this creates a vehicle to gain access to the human experts and content knowledge across the enterprise simultaneously.

- **Coupled Environments:** These provide secure enterprise-to-enterprise SKME connections across organizational boundaries. Although this can be a complex undertaking, having an integrated environment offers exposure to materials that open up solution selling across brands. To accomplish this requires robust design associated with your access management capabilities. Below is a simple Venn diagram that highlights the exponential nature of the complexity related to fine-grained access requirements for coupled environments.

Access Management in Coupled Environments

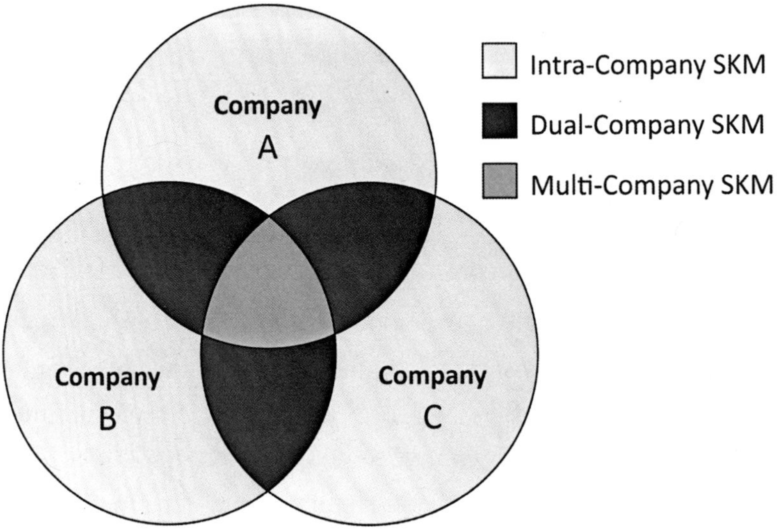

The example provides context for three companies, but as you extrapolate additional communities being tied in, the access rights become increasingly complex. Within one environment (Intra- Company), you only need to consider content with internal roles. As you add Multi-Company community integration, it becomes increasingly important to manage access to content across roles from the various companies. There may be a need to segment content to specific groups or individuals across companies. Remember, as you define roles and access rights you must not only consider access requirements internally, but also across company boundaries to understand specific alignment requirements.

Company compliance and confidentiality standards will demand a clearly articulated and well-designed access management capability to mitigate the potential for unintended information access. Moreover, you are not dealing with just one company standard; you will be required to balance the requirements of two or more company standards.

Depending on the objective of your organization, this list of opportunities for future advancement of your SKME may vary. It is first important to build a solid foundation based on your core business needs before expanding the breadth of your SKME as outlined in the early chapters of this book. When appropriate, you may include some of these ideas into the scope of your SKME initiative.

The Future of Shared Social Content

Now, as a final topic, let's expand our thoughts on the future of Social Knowledge Management and consider what it will mean to you professionally and personally.

What will social knowledge mean 10 to 15 years from now? Just consider what is happening today:

- You are *Googled*: Before you have a meeting with somebody you have most probably searched to find more information about the person. And they most assuredly have done the same thing regarding you.

- Social Network Perceptions: How often have you heard that someone was not granted an interview, not hired, or fired due to an inappropriate post or some other online missive?
- Credit Score and Identity Theft: The haunting credit score that holds many back from their wants and needs. Or the potential of having your identify stolen and virtual reputation ruined.
- Exaggerated vs. Proven Expertise: Ability to query on specific expertise before even meeting or talking to an individual through professional networking sites.

Now let's consider the future. Will the concept of a resume be a thing of the past? A host of attributes that represent you exist today in the cloud, some are readily accessible, and some are not. But even today, people can usually glean a perception of you by searching the Internet. Now think about where it will be in 10 to 15 years. Individuals will likely have a *Unified Reputation Profile,* which may consolidate an individual's attributes, and could be accessible by essentially anyone that is interested. It will become increasingly important to manage your social reputation, as it will become your de facto identity.

Rather than doing a Google search and clicking on various links of disparate information, individuals will have a reputation profile that will include this information. At best, you *may* be able to influence the content. This truly becomes a situation in which *your reputation precedes you*. Even today, there are social scoring mechanisms that rate and rank your influence within the social world on the Internet. Now imagine all social and non-social elements being linked together, ending up becoming a virtual representation of you.

Unified Reputation

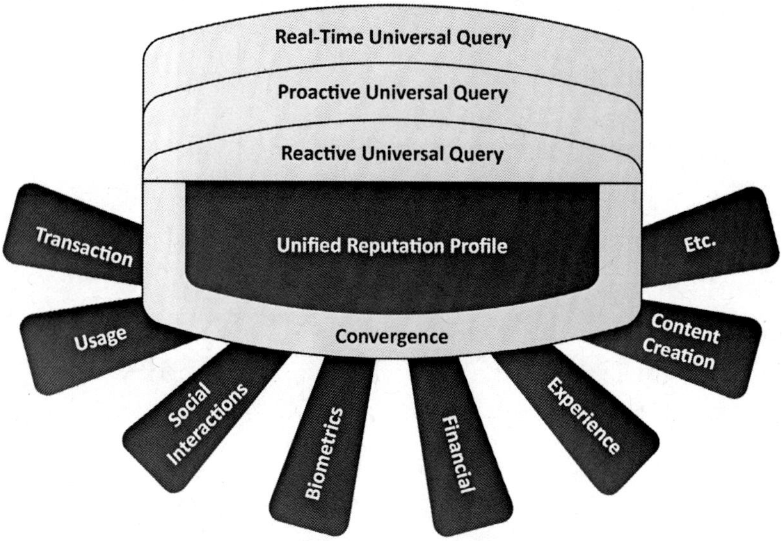

A Unified Reputation Profile will include elements about your transactions, application usage, social interactions, biometrics, financial, work experience, knowledge creation, etc. As the various attributes that make up your profile are linked and combined, people will have access to a holistic view of *you* within a single view. There will be privacy considerations, to be sure, but the level of detail available for this type of profile is surprising, even today.

This information will be accessible reactively, proactively, and in real-time. This will introduce the opportunity to create matching algorithms that will *connect* people and content based on your profile, location, and any number of other attributes. Think about being at a conference and attempting to network with others with similar interests. It is often hard to connect with the right people with common interests randomly in an ocean of people. Now think about opting-in with your profile to help facilitate connections. Based on what you want, the profiles can help you connect in a way that was not possible before.

Think about where new inventions like Google Glass™ will take us in the *social* space. Google Glass™ is a wearable technology that utilizes an optical head mounted display (OHMD) that presents information in thin air in a smartphone–like, hands-free format. It can take pictures with a wink of an eye and show a walking route displayed visually in front of you while you walk. In 10 years, what we think of as a smartphone could very well be replaced by all sorts of Google Glass™–like wearable devices that become our landscape (some would consider this an invasive technology, requiring a physical unplugging to see the trees and life on earth going on around you), or our vehicle to exchange information and ideas without even one word uttered (smartphones have social apps but wearable devices could become a part of how you navigate the world and would be completely hands free!). How social do you want to be? You can display your profile to everyone you meet in the coffee shop also wearing their device… Are you single? Looking for a job? What are your credentials? All of this and more can be conveyed with a wink!

In the future, we believe the idea of unification of data and content will be easily accessible *socially* and new ways to access and convey information will be enabled through technologies initiated via a simple wink.

Social Knowledge Management is a discipline that has found its roots in the enterprise, making it more effective to share, retain, and iterate knowledge assets. This has shown to have tremendous value, and is a catalyst that is driving dramatic change in how we manage our corporate knowledge assets. In the future you will see this concept expand into a broader capability that impacts people professionally and personally. It will be important to manage all aspects of knowledge within and outside the enterprise.

Reflecting on Our Journey, and Your Road Forward

As discussed in Chapter 1, social knowledge has always been a part of human society, a part of who we are. It is only recently that social knowledge could be captured, retained, shared, and iterated across a broad community with a new generation of collaborative and knowledge management technologies and capabilities.

In the past, much of the valuable social interactions that take place within the enterprise simply perished upon the conclusion of a conversation or interaction. Or, at the very best, it was captured within a particular information silo (email, database, IM, human). With Social Knowledge Management, the new technologies and processes available to an enterprise enable the ability to retain once evasive social knowledge into an essential part of corporate memory.

Techniques and methods described in this book provide a roadway to pursue your own Social Knowledge Management journey. The road will be challenging and full of surprises, yet ultimately beneficial to the enterprise and rewarding to the team that pursues it. Taking advantage of new technologies, adding some unique processes, methods, and a *human touch* will incite a truly innovative environment. This will spark the creation of new ideas along the way, both professionally and personally.

You have taken your first step along the road to Social Knowledge Management by reading this book. Now be part of the future by visiting *www.socialknowledgemanagement.com* to access the latest information and, most importantly, to share your ideas and thoughts. Become a part of the future of SKM by *sharing your knowledge.*

Quick List: How do you know when you are in the express lane?

You are ready to expand the breadth of you SKM scope when:

People are coming to you for advice and counsel regarding SKM.

You notice your organization is starting to have a better *corporate memory.*

The organization's culture changes from one of *bouncing* from trend to trend to one of *adopting and proving.*

Step by Step: Want to try something today?

Follow this process:

1. List the areas where SKM has impacted the workflow in the organization.
2. Tell your Social Knowledge story! Remember, *Conversations build Communities!*

Authors

Kenneth E. Russell, PhD

Twitter: @DrKenRussell

Dr. Kenneth E. Russell is focused on transforming the Applied Technology Acceleration Institute (ATAI) at Wichita State University (WSU) into a research facility with leading edge approaches and methods designed to increase industry partnerships and complement/accelerate the impact of technology/technology consumption at the new Innovation Campus at WSU. In addition, he represents Wichita State University as a senior technology and organization leader and works to build executive level relationships, particularly in the areas of Enterprise Strategy, Intellectual Capital, and EpiData Insight.

His experience includes developing and implementing enterprise programs (Enterprise Strategy, Organizational Leadership, Change Management, Enterprise Architecture, Bioinformatics), and forging necessary relationships with Legal, IT, Senior Leadership, and Lines of Business to ensure necessary commitments for success. Dr. Russell leads with a combination of technology expertise, organizational acumen, and a keen understanding of the importance of precise communication and practical governance. He leverages coaching and mentoring to assist with behavior and culture change efforts (including organization architecture, situational leadership, leader vs. manager, and communication skills coaching).

The new Applied Technology Acceleration Institute (ATAI) will continue to build upon existing work and industry partnerships while working to increase capabilities, incentives, and opportunities for partners, industry, faculty, and student workers. Several foundational Centers of Innovation have been created to lead the way in the areas of: Technology Consumption, Social Knowledge, Dynamic Data, and Commercialization.

Prior to WSU, Dr. Russell led the Intellectual Capital Transformation effort at Cisco, where he and his team received the 2014 Forrester Groundswell award for most innovative service of the year. He was Chief Information Officer for the David H. Murdock Research Institute (DHMRI) in Kannapolis, North Carolina where he provided executive leadership to drive delivery and execution of the technology requirements for developing and implementing a green-field life sciences research facility. His experience also includes several years as director of IT Strategy & Consulting with Duke Energy, leader of the Enterprise Architecture program at Bank of America, as well as technology and strategy engagements with Fortune 500 organizations (including financial services, healthcare, manufacturing, and retail), academic institutions, non- profits, and innovative startup companies.

Renée La Londe

Twitter: @relalonde

Renée has 20 years of experience in the high-tech industry. In the past nine years, as the CEO of iTalent Corporation, she has been instrumental in growing revenues by more than 100 percent year-over-year. She has put together an outstanding executive management team and has driven key initiatives such as creating consulting practices around eService, Web Services, Oracle ERP, Business Intelligence, SKM, and Change Management.

iTalent Corporation's innovation in the SKM space won "Best in Biz 2014 International Gold Award as Most Innovative Service of the Year."

Prior to iTalent Corporation, Renée held many senior-level positions in eService and eCommerce at Fortune 500 companies such as Apple, Cisco, and NetApp. At NetApp for six years, as a Sr. Director of eService, she led major system deployments around online customer support including building out, from the ground up, the company's award-winning online support site (NOW: NetApp On the Web). She holds a BA from the University of Texas, in Austin and is a Texas Exes Life Member (Hook'em Horns!). She is frequently asked to speak and blog on current technology trends and women in technology.

Fred Walters

Twitter: @FredSKM

Fred has over 25 years of experience in high-tech, leading transformative initiatives in the Silicon Valley. In the early 90s he led Apple's first client-server online order (pre-Internet), and later moved on to deliver Apple's first package implementation of ERP and CRM. In the late 90s, Fred joined his technology peer from Apple to help deliver Cisco's initial Internet Commerce capabilities. In the early 2000s, Fred recognized the opportunity related to "on-demand" capabilities and co-founded a company that was an inaugural partner of Salesforce.com's initial AppExchange release. Fred has been a partner at iTalent since 2007 where he has led innovative Shared Services engagements in both IT and Operations for Cisco. He is now excited to be part of his next transformative effort – iTalent's Social Knowledge Management Practice. Fred holds a BS in Business Management from San Jose State University.

Acknowledgements

Fabio Bergamo

Fabio Bergamo is an experienced futurist with a passion for Knowledge Management. He has a Computer Science BS, an MBA from the University of Massachusetts, and over 17 years of experience working for multiple Fortune 500 companies in the network technology field. Fabio is focused on Business Process Reengineering with a strong emphasis on Change Management/ Transformation. With the understanding that the only constant in life is change, and that technology tools come and go, Fabio believes the key to success is to focus on business outcomes while addressing the physiological challenges derived from technology evolutions and market transitions, therefore the interest to lead the way in the evolution of Social Knowledge Management.

Sherman Chan

Sherman Chan is a data connoisseur, enjoying a sip of data every chance he gets. He has traveled different industries, sampling the finest data that is out there – sales, finance, banking, healthcare, pharmaceuticals, biological, social, retail, etc. Along his travels, he has encountered many data types, even living among them and understanding their meaning and purpose of their existence, eventually becoming ONE with them. He has helped transform shy data into vibrant and colorful displays to drive Social Knowledge Management performance and better decision-making.

Juana Dehanov

Juana Dehanov is a go-getter by nature, relentlessly bringing structure and agility to any project she tackles. Juana is an experienced Social Knowledge Worker; her background includes an Engineering Degree in Computer Science, an MBA, and experience deploying and managing Social Knowledge Management Environments. Juana is a skillful traveler who backpacked around the world for one year. This experience allowed Juana to expand her horizons and connect with new cultures. Juana's motto is "the only thing that's constant in life is change" so you might as well embrace it and run with it!

Jason Hurst

Jason Hurst enjoys developing innovative products that provide engaging and streamlined user experiences. He has managed the development of several products that were successful in very competitive markets, attracting new customers and playing a vital role in the success of the company or business unit. As a manager of a variety of software and web development projects, he understands the requirements necessary for establishing robust and interactive Social Knowledge Management Environments. Thankfully, his cats often volunteer to help.

Raju Kotha

Raju Kotha has 15 years of experience managing large application, infrastructure, and mobile development/improvement projects for Fortune 500 companies. Raju led complex cross-functional Web and Social Knowledge Management Projects. His experience as an Architect for Social Web has created successful SKM Solutions across the globe. Raju has a Masters in Software Engineering and undergraduate degree in Mathematics, a combination that helps him bring reason and logic to everything that he does.

Leslie Ottavi

Leslie Ottavi's 20-plus year career in high-tech, highlighted by her leadership in driving change, positions businesses to be ready, willing, and able to embrace new business processes and technologies. As part of iTalent's team, Leslie has led Fortune 100 enterprise-wide change management and enterprise collaboration (social) initiatives. Whether running strategic business development programs or transforming people, processes, and technology to ensure operational excellence, Leslie is passionate about achieving results through strong customer, partner, and team relationships.

Rudy Peters

Rudy Peters is a results -oriented information technology leader with over 18 years of comprehensive business, technical, and Social Knowledge Management experience. He has a proven ability to manage diverse projects and teams simultaneously. He enjoys working collaboratively with teams and is capable of understanding business clients and technical colleague's requirements with the ability to act as their liaison, successfully fostering bi-directional communication between groups. He is a strategic thinker and is always looking for ways to reassess/reengineer processes to make them more efficient.

Valerie Risch

Valerie Risch is an accomplished technology leader offering business development and innovation via technology planning, management, and architecture consulting. She is a Social Knowledge Practice Leader and her experience includes several years of technology and strategy engagements with Fortune 100 organizations. She demonstrates precise technology and business acumen, understands the value of process management, and possesses an ability to lead efforts in situations of ambiguity, shifts in technology, and organizational change.

Becky Scott

Becky Scott could be called a "social media addict" since she lives and breathes social media and community. In reality, she is quite passionate about bringing brands and their customers together. Becky has a varied background that includes technical project management, marketing, editing, and writing. Becky has managed online communities for 15 years and social properties since Live Journal was a "thing" and Facebook required university emails. She honed her writing and editing skills on sites like AOL's Aisle Dash, Ask Patty, Tree.com, and ucsd.edu.

Austens Thompson

Austens Thompson recently graduated from UC Santa Cruz with a BS in Technology and Information Management. He works to manage and maintain Social Knowledge Management environments and leverages data to gain insight about these communities. He actively engages with the community and runs competitions to gamify and push the boundaries of collaboration and social knowledge.

Julie Valentine

Julie Valentine is passionate about bringing people and technology together to solve real-life challenges. She has worked with various corporate clients to implement strategies to empower thinkers, doers, and makers to build a more vibrant world through technology. She has worked with companies like Hewlett Packard, Applied Materials, and Cisco for the past 15+ years to steward large-scale technology implementations and develops successful engagement strategies.

Index

Q

R

S